TO BE LIKE JESUS

40 Meditations for Your Journey toward Christlikeness

Some books focus on what Christ has done *for us*, and others on what Christ does *in us*. Rare, however, are books that teach us how Christ works *in us* on the basis of what he had already accomplished *for us*. Brian Hedges has written one of these rare books, laid out in short devotions crafted to stimulate faith that bears fruit through love. This is a book not only to read, but to practice in the pursuit of holiness.

Dr. Joel R. Beeke
President, Puritan Reformed Theological Seminary, Grand Rapids, Michigan

TO BE LIKE JESUS

40 Meditations for Your Journey toward Christlikeness

BRIAN G. HEDGES

To Be Like Jesus

© 2020 Brian Hedges

ISBN:
Print: 978-1-63342-189-9
epub: 978-1-63342-190-5
mobi: 978-1-63342-191-2

Shepherd Press
P.O. Box 24
Wapwallopen, PA 18660

www.shepherdpress.com

Typography by **documen** www.documen.co.uk

Dedication

To my father-in-law,
Marion C. Ivey Jr.
and in loving memory
of my mother-in-law,
Linda Ivey.

To "be away from the body"
is to be "at home with the Lord."
(2 Corinthians 5:8)

Acknowledgments

I WISH TO EXPRESS MY THANKS to Shepherd Press for the opportunity to repurpose material from my first book, *Christ Formed in You*, for this new devotional. My hope is that readers will view *To Be Like Jesus* as a supplement, rather than a replacement, to the earlier book. Thanks especially to Jim Holmes for his help in shepherding this project through to completion.

No acknowledgments would be complete without expressing my love for my beautiful wife, Holly, and our four children, Stephen, Matthew, Susannah, and Abby. Holly, my admiration for you just grows year by year. Thank you for saying yes in 1996 and for journeying with me on this great adventure. Stephen, when I first started writing books, you were a little boy; now you are a man. I can hardly believe how fast time flies, but I am so proud of the man you have become. Keep following Jesus and never lose your enthusiasm for life, laughter, and music. Matt, I admire your love for truth and your passion for learning. In your reading of much deeper books on theology, church history, and apologetics, I hope my little books will also spur you on in your pursuit of God. Suz, life is so much more fun with you around! Thank you for the many ways you brighten our days. Abby Taylor, you bring so much joy and happiness to our family! Thank you for giving me so many hugs.

I have dedicated this book to my father-in-law, Marion C. Ivey Jr., and in loving memory of my mother-in-law, Linda, who went to be with the Lord on October 19, 2020. Linda was an exemplary wife and mother, and a vibrant Christian with a deep prayer life. We will miss her deeply. But we do not sorrow as those who have no hope, for we know she is in her Savior's presence, and that we will be reunited with her on resurrection morning, when Christ makes all things new. Marion, I'm deeply grateful for the beautiful daughter you raised so well and the enduring legacy of your faithful love to Linda, your abiding trust in the Lord, and your godly example to our family.

The Lord Jesus Christ has been immeasurably kind to me. If I received what I deserved, I would have been in hell a long time ago. Instead, he has redeemed me by his precious blood, given me a seat at his banqueting table, and a place of belonging in the Father's family. Thank you, Lord Jesus, for your unfathomable mercy.

Contents

Introduction

THE CHRISTIAN LIFE is a journey of spiritual and moral transformation into the glorious image and likeness of God's Son, the Lord Jesus Christ. This journey is lifelong. We begin this journey when we first believe in Jesus, but will not reach our final destination until the final resurrection, when our bodies will be raised, transformed, and glorified, as we are fully and finally conformed to the image of Christ.

As with any lengthy journey, sometimes Christians lose their way. We can become disoriented and confused. We mistake the terrain we have already traversed, lose sight of the road on which we tread, and forget the destination to which we travel. Sometimes we take detours. Or we get stuck on the side of the road. All of us sometimes need help.

This little book is a series of 40 devotional readings, designed to help in a specific way. These readings are lightly edited excerpts from my larger book *Christ Formed in You: The Power of the Gospel for Personal Change. Christ Formed in You* functioned as something of a map for the journey, charting out a comprehensive theology of sanctification. *To Be Like Jesus,* on the other hand, is more like a series of encouraging road signs—brief meditations to help you in your journey toward Christlikeness.

Each meditation begins with Scripture and ends with questions for reflection and a brief prayer. My goal throughout has been to anchor your faith in the power of grace and the hope of the gospel: to set your gaze on the glorious good news of what God has done in sending his Son to redeem us, and his Spirit to renew us. My hope is that, as you read, you will be drawn into closer fellowship with Christ himself, even as you are conformed more and more to his image.

Soli Deo Gloria

Brian G. Hedges
October 2020

Day 1

The Chief End of Man

So God created man in his own image, in the
image of God he created him; male and female
he created them.
(Genesis 1:27)

WHY DID GOD CREATE US? For what purpose? The Westminster
Shorter Catechism answers, "Man's chief end is to glorify God and
enjoy him forever."[1] Speaking originally of the scattered exiles of
Israel whom God promised to redeem, Isaiah 43:6–7 agrees:

I will say to the north, Give up,
 and to the south, Do not withhold;
bring my sons from afar
 and my daughters from the end of the earth,
everyone who is called by my name,
 whom I created for my glory,
 whom I formed and made.

In the first chapter of Genesis we don't read that man was created
for God's glory, but in God's image. What's the difference? Not much.
As Sinclair Ferguson has noted, "In Scripture, image and glory are
interrelated ideas. As the image of God, man was created to reflect,
express, and participate in the glory of God, in miniature, creaturely
form."[2] The Heidelberg Catechism agrees, "God created man good,
and after his own image, in true righteousness and holiness, that he

---

1 *Westminster Shorter Catechism*, Question 1: "What is the chief end of man?"
2 Sinclair B. Ferguson, *The Holy Spirit* (Downers Grove, IL: InterVarsity Press, 1996) 139-
 140.

might rightly know God his Creator, heartily love him and live with him in eternal happiness to glorify and praise him."[3]

God created human beings in his image so that they would glorify him by rightly representing him. In other words, the more we resemble God, the better we honor him. With this in mind, look at Genesis 1:26–27.

Then God said, "Let us make man in our image, after our likeness. And let them have dominion over the fish of the sea and over the birds of the heavens and over the livestock and over all the earth and over every creeping thing that creeps on the earth." So God created man in his own image, in the image of God he created him; male and female he created them.

Human beings were God's crowning achievement in creation. We alone are made in God's image, after his likeness. Our creation alone was prefaced with the transcript of God's consultation within himself: "Let us make man in our image." For the creation of everything else Scripture simply records God's words, "Let there be . . . and it was so." But man and woman were different. We were designed and commissioned by God with a special assignment in creation: to display God. As the early church father Irenaeus said, "The glory of God is man fully alive, and the life of man is the vision of God."[4]

Reflection Questions

- What does it mean to be created for God's glory?
- Does your life display God?
- What do you think Irenaeus meant in saying "The glory of God is man fully alive"?

---

3 The Heidelberg Catechism, Question 6: "Did God then create man so wicked and perverse?"

4 Irenaeus, *Against Heresies*, Book IV, Chapter 20, Number 7. Quoted in Ben Patterson, *Deepening Your Conversation with God: Learning to Love to Pray* (Minneapolis, MN: Bethany House Publishers, 2001) 87.

Prayer

Great God of the Universe,

To be created in your image and made for your glory is an inconceivable wonder, an inestimable privilege! Help me to grasp the special dignity that you have given to me as your image-bearer. Help me to display your glory in my life today.

Amen.

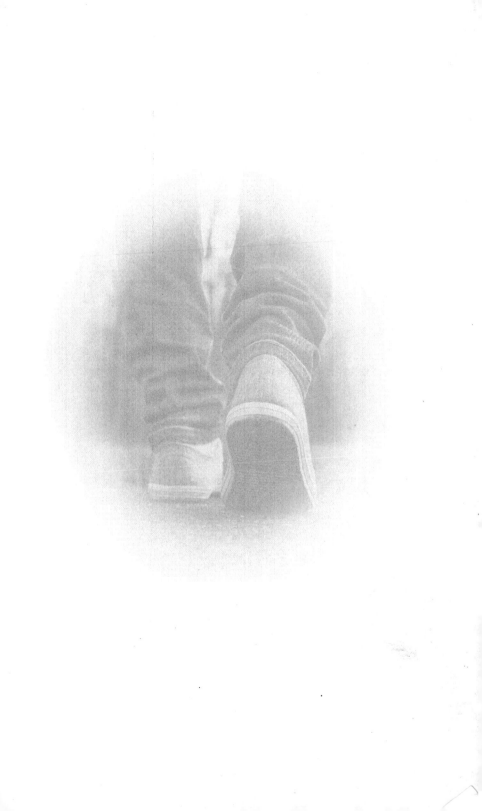

Day 2
Created for Relationships

It is not good that man should be alone.

(Genesis 2:8)

To be created in the image of God means we are designed to display God's nature, character, and glory. As a mirror is made for reflection, so God created us to be mirrors of his character, instruments for reflecting his glory.

Created in God's image, we are invested with special dignity and entrusted with particular duties. Our distinct worth as human beings springs from being God's image-bearers, the unique reflectors of his character on earth. The rest of creation *declares* God's glory, speaking of it vividly in a great variety of ways (Ps. 19:1). But we *reflect* it, actually making it, in small part, visible and tangible.

One of the supreme ways we reflect God's glory is by relating to other human beings in God-honoring ways. We ascribe glory to God's name by reflecting his character to others. As Anthony Hoekema writes, "We should not think of the image of God only as a noun but also as a verb: we are to *image* God by the way we live, and the heart of the image of God is love for God and for others."[1]

To be God's image-bearers means we are created for relationships. This is implied in Genesis 1:26–27: "Then God said, 'Let us make man in our image, after our likeness.' So God created man in his own image, in the image of God he created him; male and female he created them."

Why does the text connect being created in God's image with being created male and female? Not because God himself is both masculine and feminine—he is unequivocally masculine. It is because God himself is a community—a trinity of persons, existing in eternal

1 Anthony A. Hoekema, *Created in God's Image* (Grand Rapids, MI: William B. Eerdmans Publishing Co., 1986) 52.

self-giving love. In creating man and woman together, he created a community. God created man to image his glory, but his glory could not be adequately displayed by an individual living in isolation from others. God himself says in Genesis 2:18, "It is not good that man should be alone." As John Ortberg writes,

> Community is rooted in the being of God. . . . The Trinity exists as a kind of eternal dance of joyful love among Father, Son, and Spirit. . . . God created human beings because he was so in love with community that he wanted a world full of people to share it with. He wanted to invite them all to the dance. And life within the Trinity was to be the pattern for our lives.[2]

At the core of our nature as God's image-bearers, we are *relational* beings. This involves a threefold relationship: "between man and God, between man and his fellowmen, and between man and nature."[3]

Reflection Questions

- What is at the heart of imaging God?
- Have you ever thought about relationships in light of the Trinity?
- Are there any relationships in your life that need special attention today?

Prayer

Father, Son, and Holy Spirit, Eternal Three-in-One God,

Thank you for creating me in your image and giving me the capacity to love. You are love and I will never truly know love until I truly know you. I want to know you more. Help me today to live in the light of your love. And fill my heart with your love, that I might love others.

Amen.

---

2 John Ortberg, *Everybody's Normal Till You Get to Know Them* (Grand Rapids, MI: Zondervan, 2003) 34, 35, 39.

3 Hoekema, *Created in God's Image*, 75.

Day 3

The Godwardness of Sin

Against you, you only, have I sinned and done
what is evil in your sight.
(Psalm 51:4)

THOUGH WE ARE CREATED IN THE IMAGE OF GOD, the tragic reality is that we have rebelled against God and now live under his judgment and wrath (Gen. 3:16–19; Rom. 1:18). The image of God is therefore distorted. In Calvin's words, God's image is deformed, vitiated, mutilated, maimed, disease-ridden, and disfigured.[1]

This is true for all of us. "All have sinned and fall short of the glory of God" (Rom. 3:23). We have failed to glorify God by not loving his person, obeying his laws, and delighting in his glory. Rather than exclusively worshiping our glorious Creator, we have served and worshiped created things (Rom. 1:21–23). We are "alienated from the life of God" and "dead in trespasses and sins" (Eph. 4:18; 2:1). The image of God within us has become so marred and distorted that each of us, without exception, fails to display his character in fullness.

But we don't realize the gravity of this evil. Our souls are so calloused by sin that we do not sense its infinite offensiveness to God. J. I. Packer observes that the biblical words for "sin" portray it

in a variety of different ways: as rebellion against our
rightful owner and ruler; as transgression of the bounds he
set; as missing the mark he told us to aim at; as breaking
the law he enacted; as defiling (dirtying, polluting) ourselves
in his sight, so making o urselves unfit for his company; as
embracing folly by shutting our ears to his wisdom; and as
incurring guilt before his judgment seat.[2]

---

1 See references in Hoekema, *Created in God's Image*, 83.
2 J. I. Packer, *Rediscovering Holiness* (Ann Arbor, MI: Vine Books, 1992) 50.

These pictures reveal several distinct aspects of our sin, but the common denominator they share is their *Godwardness*. All sin—even so-called little sins—are evil because they are ultimately committed against our infinitely holy God. When we sin against God we spurn his honor, preferring other things to his glory. Even when we sin against other human beings, we simultaneously assault God's glory by hurting those who bear his image. James condemns us for using our tongues to curse others because they are "people who are made in the likeness of God" (James 3:9).

David committed adultery with Bathsheba, murdered her husband, and covered his sin so the public would not know. Yes, these were grievous and horrible sins against people, but David's confession to God reveals his deeper understanding. They were not just sins against people. They were sins against God: violations of his law, infractions of his will, assaults on those who bore his image, and therefore, on God himself. That is why David confessed, "Against you, you only, have I sinned and done what is evil in your sight" (Ps. 51:4).

Every sin against a human being is also a sin against God. Egotism, lust, bitterness, gossip, slander, racial prejudice, violence, the devaluing of human life—these are sins against God's image-bearers, and therefore sins against God himself.

Reflection Questions

- Why are your sins against people also sins against God?

- Take inventory right now: how have you fallen short of God's glory?

Prayer

Almighty God,

Please help me to view my sins in a Godward way. Help me to see that all of my sins are distortions of your glorious image and violations of your perfect will.

Amen.

Day 4

Glorious Ruins

All have sinned and fall short of the glory of God.
(Romans 3:23)

THE CONSEQUENCES OF SIN are devastating, damaging each of the three relationships for which we were created—that is, relationships humans have with God, one another, and nature.

We see these consequences in Genesis 3, following the sin of the first man and woman. Before sin, they had enjoyed unbroken friendship with God. But after their sinful rebellion, they hid from him in shame and fear, trying without success to cover their shame with fig leaves (Gen. 3:7–10). Before sin, they had also enjoyed the only perfect marriage that ever existed (Gen. 2:21–25). But following that fatal taste of the forbidden fruit, their relationship was characterized by shame, blame-shifting, and conflict (Gen. 3:7, 12, 16). Before sin, they lived in paradise—a perfect environment. But ever since, humans have lived in conflict with a world under God's curse (Gen. 3:17–19).

- Sin alienates us from God, leaving us spiritually dead, enslaved to our passions, and subject to God's just wrath (Eph. 2:1–3; 4:18–19).

- Sin also brings conflict into human relationships: between husbands and wives; parents and children; and people of different races, languages, and nations.

- Sin is also what put us in conflict with the created order. Originally a welcoming environment, the earth is now hostile to human life in significant ways. Natural disasters, environmental devastation, and the harshness of the elements are just some of the consequences of our rebellion against God.

So, do human beings still bear God's image, given the extent of sin's devastation? The answer is Yes . . . sort of. Genesis 5:1–3 and 9:6—both written of the post-Fall world—echo Genesis 1:26–28 by indicating that we do continue to bear God's image. But as Calvin said, "Even though we grant that God's image was not totally annihilated and destroyed in him, yet it was so corrupted that whatever remains is frightful deformity."[1] A trace of his image is still present, but not enough for people to rightly perceive his glory and give him the honor he deserves. Alistair Begg provides a helpful illustration:

> One of the charming aspects of touring in Scotland is the discovery, often in remote regions, of ancient castles. While some of them are occupied, many of them are now in ruins. But they continue to attract our attention and cause us to pause in wonder because, although they have fallen into disrepair, there is still a grandeur to them. Ruins they may be, but they are still possessed of enough of their former dignity to be justifiably regarded as "glorious ruins." So it is with man. As offensive as it may seem to be, the Bible says that we are ruins! On account of sin, God's image in us has been obscured, but not obliterated.[2]

We humans are amazing in our ability to imitate the Creator in countless ways: composing symphonies; painting beautiful landscapes; building cathedrals, skyscrapers, and bridges; and sending explorers into space. But as magnificent as these accomplishments are, they fall far short of God's intention, when done without regard for his honor and glory. We are glorious ruins! Tiny flashes of light flicker in our achievements. But these are merely distorted glimmers of glory in the broken shards of our fallen, fragmented world.

---

1 John Calvin, John T. McNeil, ed., Ford L. Battles, trans., *Institutes of the Christian Religion,* Book I, Chap. XV, 4 (Philadelphia, PA: The Westminster Press, 1960) 189.
2 Alistair Begg, *What Angels Wish They Knew: The Basics of True Christianity* (Chicago, IL: Moody Press, 1998) 37.

Reflection Questions

- In what ways do we still see the divine image in fallen human beings?

- How has the fall tainted and corrupted even the best that human beings can do?

- In what ways could your life be described as "glorious ruins"?

Prayer

How great you have made us and how far we have fallen, O God! You have made us for yourself, to be like yourself, to display your glorious character. And yet, we have turned against you, using the capacities you have given us to defy you. Forgive us—forgive me—for our treason, O God. And restore me to your glory.

Amen.

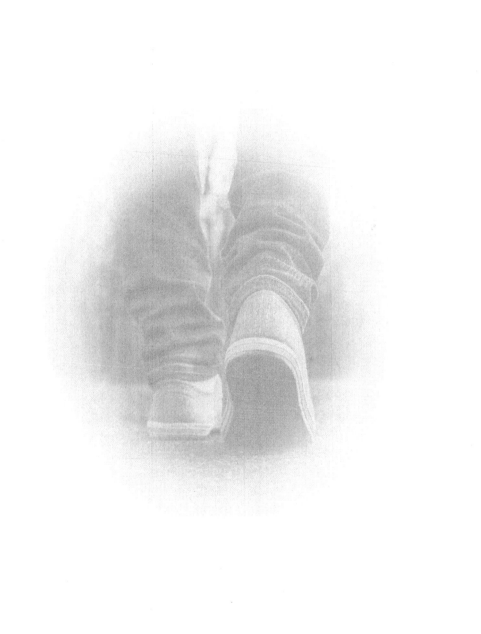

Day 5

The Gracious Rescue

> Grace to you and peace from God our Father and the
> Lord Jesus Christ, who gave himself for our sins to deliver
> us from the present evil age, according to the will of
> our God and Father, to whom be glory forever and ever.
> Amen.
> (Galatians 1:3–5)

THE GOOD NEWS IS THAT GOD has formed a rescue plan. Not willing to abandon his creation to evil, God has purposed to redeem and restore the world by setting a new people apart for himself.

Although hints of this plan are given even before the expulsion of Adam and Eve from the Garden (Gen. 3:15), God's redemptive mission truly began to take shape when he called Abraham. God promised to give Abraham two things: a son (and descendants) through whom the world would be blessed (Gen. 12:1–3), and a special land that would belong to his heirs forever (Gen. 17:7–8). The promised son was Isaac. The descendants were the children of Israel. The land would be Canaan. God later rescued this people from slavery in Egypt and consecrated them as a special nation (Ex. 1–15) over which he himself would reign as sovereign king (Ex. 19:3–6; Num. 23:21; Deut. 33:2–5).

Once Canaan was settled, God promised David, the greatest of Israel's earthly kings, a son who would be forever enthroned over his people (2 Sam. 7). The entire story of the Old Testament is the outworking of these two covenant promises to Abraham and David. It is the story of God's glory gradually returning to earth through this people, chosen and redeemed to bear his image.

Israel, however, failed to reflect the glory of the Lord as they should. Israel's history in Scripture is marked by repeated cycles of rebellion against God, exile from God, and deliverance by God. In spite of God's grace and longsuffering, the hearts of the people continually turned to idols instead of their Covenant Lord. God repeatedly sent prophets to denounce their rebellion and idolatry, warning of the impending judgment that would surely fall upon them. They usually refused to listen. But a kernel of hope was buried in the prophets' oracles of doom. God promised that he would not utterly forsake his people. He would preserve a remnant of people to whom he would faithfully fulfill his promises (Isa. 6:9–13; 10:20–22). He would send a suffering servant to lead the people in a second exodus (Isa. 40–66). And he would create a new world (Isa. 65–66).

This rescue plan comes to fruition in Jesus, the son of David, the son of Abraham (Matt. 1:1). Born in fulfillment of God's promises (Matt. 1:18–25), Jesus is the ultimate descendant of Abraham, the heir to David's throne, and the remnant of Israel (Gal. 3:16; Rom. 1:3). Jesus is the suffering servant who, through death and resurrection, ransoms God's people, inaugurates his saving reign, and ushers in the new creation (Mark 1:15; 10:45; 2 Cor. 5:17). As the great theologian Herman Bavinck summarized, "The essence of the Christian religion consists in this, that the creation of the Father, devastated by sin, is restored in the death of the Son of God, and re-created by the Holy Spirit into a kingdom of God."[1]

Reflection Questions

- Have you ever read the Old Testament as the record of God's rescue plan?
- How did Jesus fulfill God's rescue plan?
- Have you trusted in Jesus for rescue?

Prayer

What amazing grace and love you have shown, Father!
Thank you for not abandoning the human race. Thank you
for devising a plan of rescue and redemption. Thank you for
sending your Son to rescue me.
Amen.

---

1 Herman Bavinck, John Bolt, gen. ed., John Vriend, trans., *Reformed Dogmatics: Volume 1: Prolegomena* (Grand Rapids, MI: Baker Academic, 2003) 112.

Day 6

New Man, New Creation

Thus it is written, "The first man Adam became a living being";
the last Adam became a life-giving spirit. But it is not the spiritual
that is first but the natural, and then the spiritual. The first man
was from the earth, a man of dust; the second man is from
heaven. As was the man of dust, so also are those who are of the
dust, and as is the man of heaven, so also are those who are of
heaven. Just as we have borne the image of the man of dust, we
shall also bear the image of the man of heaven.
(1 Corinthians 15:45–49)

IN CONTRAST TO ADAM, the first man, Jesus, came as second Adam,
the true image-bearer of God. 2 Corinthians 4:4 calls Christ, "the
image of God" and Colossians 1:15 says that he is "the image of the
invisible God, the firstborn of all creation."

Along with Hebrews 1:3, which describes the Son as the
"radiance of the glory of God and the exact imprint of his nature,"
these passages refer to the divinity of our Lord as the eternal and
preexistent Son of God. In the words of Herman Ridderbos, "When
in this context he is called . . . the Image of God, this is to say nothing
less than that in him the glory of God, indeed God himself, becomes
manifest"[1] But, as Ridderbos also observes, these passages "are in all
sorts of ways directly reminiscent of the creation story."[2] Jesus is not
only fully God, he is fully man. He comes as the second Adam, the
Last Man, the true image-bearer of God, the one who never sinned,
never failed God, never fell short.

In the unique union of deity and humanity in the person of
Jesus Christ, we therefore see not only the Word of God made flesh

---

1 Herman Ridderbos, *Paul: An Outline of His Theology* (Grand Rapids, MI: William B.
Eerdmans Publishing Co., 1975) 70.
2 Ridderbos, 70-71.

(John 1:14), but the perfect picture of what it means to be human. Jesus bears the image of God as Adam should have. The divine visage which is marred, distorted, and perverted in all other human beings, shines untarnished in him.

> Christ is called the image of God *par excellence*. . . . In Christ we see the image of God in perfection. As a skillful teacher uses visual aids to help his or her pupils understand what is being taught, so God the Father has given us in Jesus Christ a visual example of what the image of God is.[3]

Jesus Christ perfectly reflects the glory of the Father, not only because he is himself divine, but because he perfectly images God's character in his flawless humanity. In him we see what God intended all human beings to be in their relationships to God, to one another, and to creation. Consumed with a passion for his Father's glory, Jesus lived in unbroken fellowship with God. He devoted himself to loving others, his love culminating in his death as our substitute on the cross. And he commanded the winds and waves—indeed all the elements of creation—as their true Lord and rightful King.

Jesus is the true *Imago Dei*, the true image of God. But he also remakes human beings in his image through his work. His life on this earth was the perfect embodiment of all that is righteous, good, beautiful, and true. In his spotless obedience and sacrificial death, he took our place—living the life we should have lived and dying the death we should have died. And in his resurrection and exaltation, he now reigns as the second and last Adam, the True Man, the "firstborn of many brothers" (Rom. 8:29). The clear purpose of God's saving work in Jesus is to conform us to the image of his Son. Jesus is the new man, ushering in a new creation, in us (2 Cor. 5:21).

This is the unfolding of God's eternal purpose. God has predestined those chosen in Christ (Eph. 1:4–5) to be conformed to the glorious image of Christ (Rom. 8:29). This divine goal will not be fully realized until the Lord Jesus returns from heaven to "transform our lowly body to be like his glorious body" (Phil. 3:21; *cf.* 1 John 3:2).

---

3 Hoekema, *Created in God's Image*, 72, 22.

But the restoration has already begun in the redemptive work of Christ, applied in our lives by the power of God's Spirit.

Reflection Questions

- Think about the life of Jesus. What words would you use to describe his life?

- How does Jesus' life shine as an example of true humanness?

- What does Scripture mean by calling Jesus "the last Adam"?

Prayer

Father,

Your Son, the Lord Jesus, has lived the life I should have lived and haven't. He has imaged your glory in perfection. He is the perfect picture of true humanity. Please conform me to his glorious image. Help me to become more like him. Amen.

Day 7

Becoming Like Jesus

For those whom he foreknew he also predestined to
be conformed to the image of his Son, in order that
he might be the firstborn among many brothers.
(Romans 8:29)

THE ESSENCE OF THIS HOLINESS is *likeness* to Jesus Christ—what
some theologians call "Christiformity." When we become like Jesus,
our lives reflect God's glory and we live in right relationship to God,
other people, and the world. This is the goal God destined us for, the
vocation he has called us to. This is why we are redeemed.

This also explains why Scripture calls us to imitate Christ.
In 1 Corinthians 11:1, Paul says, "Be imitators of me, as I am of
Christ." In Ephesians 5:1–2, he writes, "Therefore be imitators
of God, as beloved children. And walk in love, as Christ loved
us and gave himself up for us, a fragrant offering and sacrifice to
God." And in Philippians 2:5–11 he urges us to have the mind of
Christ, expressed in humility and selfless service to others. The
Apostle John also exhorts us to follow Christ's example, walking as
he walked (1 John 2:6), practicing righteousness as he is righteous
(1 John 2:29, 3:7), purifying ourselves as he is pure (1 John 3:3), and
loving others as he loved (1 John 3:16–18, 4:16–17).

Charles Wesley captured the heart of Christlikeness in these
prayerful words:

> O for a heart to praise my God,
> A heart from sin set free,
> A heart that always feels Thy blood
> So freely shed for me.

A heart resigned, submissive, meek,
My great Redeemer's throne,
Where only Christ is heard to speak,
Where Jesus reigns alone.

A humble, lowly, contrite, heart,
Believing, true and clean,
Which neither life nor death can part
From Christ who dwells within.

A heart in every thought renewed
And full of love divine,
Perfect and right and pure and good,
A copy, Lord, of Thine.[1]

The acid test of all spiritual formation is this: *are you becoming more like Jesus?* Ongoing transformation is possible for you. You can become more and more like Jesus Christ. But only one way: through your increasing understanding and application of the gospel.

Reflection Questions

- Are you becoming more like Jesus?
- Are the contours of your character being shaped by his image, formed in his likeness?
- Do you increasingly hate sin and love righteousness, as he already does perfectly?
- Are you growing in humility and self-giving, which he has practiced flawlessly?
- Are you making progress in loving and serving others, as he has always done in perfection?

---

1 Charles Wesley, "O For a Heart to Praise My God," 1742.

Prayer

Heavenly Father,

The reason you have saved me is to conform me to the image of your Son. Would you make my character more like his? Do whatever you need to do. Change whatever you need to change. Help me see the glory of Jesus, and through seeing, be changed by your Spirit.

Amen.

Day 8

The Key to Transformation

And we all, with unveiled face, beholding the glory
of the Lord, are being transformed into the same
image from one degree of glory to another. For this
comes from the Lord who is the Spirit.
(2 Corinthians 3:18)

SOME OF MY FAVORITE STORIES are about characters who find themselves transported into an extraordinary world through some apparently commonplace object. Lucy walks through an old wardrobe into Narnia. Milo enters The Lands Beyond through a tollbooth. Alice pushes her way through a mirror into Looking Glass Room. Neo leaves the Matrix by taking the red pill. In each adventure, something ordinary becomes a portal into a new world.

The gospel is the most astonishing and life-transforming portal of all. The good news of what God has accomplished in his crucified and risen Son is much more than mere words. Paul says it is "the power of God for salvation to everyone who believes" (Rom. 1:16). The gospel is a portal into the new world. When we gaze on the glory of Christ in the gospel, we are changed—transformed into his image by the Spirit.

Here, the word "beholding" means "to reflect as in a mirror." That which we gaze upon is "the glory of the Lord." As we gaze, we are transformed into his image. And the medium by which this transformation takes place—the mirror in which his glorious image is viewed—is the gospel.

And even if our gospel is veiled, it is veiled only to those who
are perishing. In their case the god of this world has blinded the
minds of the unbelievers, to keep them from seeing the light of
the gospel of the glory of Christ, who is the image of God. For

what we proclaim is not ourselves, but Jesus Christ as Lord, with ourselves as your servants for Jesus' sake. For God, who said, "Let light shine out of darkness," has shone in our hearts to give the light of the knowledge of the glory of God in the face of Jesus Christ.

(2 Cor. 4:3–6)

While much could be said about this passage, the main point is that God's glory, revealed in Jesus, is seen in the message of the gospel. The gospel is the mirror which reflects God's glory. The gospel is our portal to personal transformation. As Tim Keller writes,

The gospel is not just the minimum required doctrine necessary to enter the kingdom, but the way we make all progress in the kingdom. We are not justified by the gospel and then sanctified by obedience, but the gospel is the way we grow (Gal. 3:1–3) and are renewed (Col. 1:6). It is the solution to each problem, the key to each closed door, the power through every barrier (Rom. 1:16–17).[1]

Reflection Questions

- The gospel isn't just for unbelievers; it is also for believers. Why is this so?
- What do we behold when we gaze into the mirror of the gospel?

Prayer

Thank you, Father, for the good news of the gospel. Thank you that your glory is revealed in this saving message. Help me to fix my gaze on Jesus, and, as I behold him, may your Spirit transform me more and more into his image.

Amen.

---

1 Timothy Keller, "The Centrality of the Gospel," Redeemer Presbyterian Church of New York City. Available online at: http://download.redeemer.com/pdf/learn/resources/Centrality_of_the_Gospel-Keller.pdf. Accessed February 16, 2010.

Day 9

Christy Our Substitute

For I delivered to you as of first importance what
I also received: that Christ died for our sins in
accordance with the Scriptures.
(1 Corinthians 15:3)

THE CROSS IS CENTRAL in the apostolic proclamation of the gospel. Paul said to the Corinthians, "I decided to know nothing among you except Jesus Christ and him crucified" (1 Cor. 2:2). To the Galatians, he wrote: "But far be it from me to boast except in the cross of our Lord Jesus Christ, by which the world has been crucified to me, and I to the world" (Gal. 6:14).

When we meditate on the cross, our thoughts are often taken up with the details of Jesus' physical suffering. This is not inappropriate, but neither is it Paul's principal focus. When he rehearses the essential components of his message in 1 Corinthians 15, Paul highlights not the *manner* of Christ's death with a gory description of its violence and shame, but the *meaning*—its theological significance. "He died for our sins" (v. 4).

Jesus did not die for his own sins, for he had none. He had committed no crime. "For Christ also suffered once for sins, the righteous for the unrighteous, that he might bring us to God, being put to death in the flesh but made alive in the spirit" (1 Peter 3:18). The cross was more than just the execution of a Jewish prophet. It was a *substitution*. Jesus died in our place. As J. Oswald Sanders says,

> By substitution we do not mean the saving of a life by *mere assistance*, as in the throwing of a rope to a drowning man; or by the *mere risking* of one life to save another; it is the saving of one life by the *loss* of another. As substitute, Christ

took on Himself the sinner's guilt and bore its penalty in the sinner's place.[1]

Bearing shame and scoffing rude
In my place condemned he stood
Sealed my pardon with his blood
Hallelujah! What a Savior![2]

"In my place condemned he stood." This is substitution. This is the meaning of the cross.

Reflection Questions

- Why did Paul's message focus on the cross?
- Have you ever recognized your need for a substitute?
- Have you confessed your sins to God and placed your trust in Christ alone?
- Can you say with confidence, "In *my* place condemned he stood, Hallelujah! What a Savior!"?

Prayer

Father,

I have sinned and am not worthy to be called your child. But you have sent Christ Jesus into the world to save sinners. And I'm a sinner. And I now come to you, believing that Jesus took my place, bearing my sin, guilt, and shame on the cross. Receive me now, for Jesus' sake.

Amen.

---

1 J. Oswald Sanders, *The Incomparable Christ* (Chicago, IL: Moody Press, 1971) 150.
2 Philip Bliss, "Man of Sorrows," 1875.

Day 10

The Resurrection of Christ

> For I delivered to you as of first importance what
> I also received: that Christ died for our sins in
> accordance with the Scriptures, that he was buried,
> that he was raised on the third day in accordance
> with the Scriptures.
> (1 Corinthians 15:3–4)

JESUS, OF COURSE, did not remain on the cross or stay in the grave. The Christian message would not be good news if there were nothing to report beyond Good Friday. But there *is* a report. "He was raised on the third day, in accordance with the Scriptures" (1 Cor. 15:4). The news is good because Jesus is alive!

What did Paul mean when he claimed that Christ was raised? Did he simply mean the spirit of Jesus had gone to heaven after he died? That Jesus had passed into life after death? Did he mean that he and others had seen visions of Jesus or had been visited by the spirit of Christ or had a sense of his abiding presence with them? If asked, as one hymn does, "You ask me how I know he lives?" would Paul have answered, "He lives within my heart"? What does resurrection mean?

First, Paul meant that the physical body of Jesus of Nazareth—the same body that was killed through crucifixion, wrapped in linens, and laid in Joseph of Arimathea's tomb—was raised out of death into glorious, *physical* life. In 1 Corinthians 15:5–8, Paul named some of the many eyewitnesses of the risen Christ (including himself) as proof. When he wrote these words, many of those witnesses were still alive.

In one appearance, Jesus ate fish with his disciples, proving the tangibility and physicality of his resurrection body (Luke 24:33–43).

As Luke says, Jesus "presented himself alive after his suffering by many proofs, appearing to [the apostles] during 40 days and speaking about the kingdom of God" (Acts 1:3). The resurrection means that the body of Jesus emerged from death in glorious triumph!

But the resurrection of Christ is not only physical; it is also eschatological. This means it belongs to, and effectively inaugurates, the age to come. This is why Paul draws the connection between the resurrection of Christ in the past and the resurrection of believers in the future.

> But in fact Christ has been raised from the dead, the firstfruits of those who have fallen asleep. For as by a man came death, by a man has come also the resurrection of the dead. For as in Adam all die, so also in Christ shall all be made alive. But each in his own order: Christ the firstfruits, then at his coming those who belong to Christ. Then comes the end, when he delivers the kingdom to God the Father after destroying every rule and every authority and power. For he must reign until he has put all his enemies under his feet. The last enemy to be destroyed is death.
>
> (1 Cor. 15:20–26)

Notice that Paul calls the resurrection of Christ "the firstfruits of those who have fallen asleep" (v. 20). This agricultural term derives its significance from the Old Testament, where worshipers brought their "firstfruits" sacrifices each year at the beginning of the spring harvest (Ex. 23:19; Lev. 23:10–11). The firstfruits offering was not only the first and best offering; it represented the entire harvest. As C. S. Lewis observes,

> The New Testament writers speak as if Christ's achievement in rising from the dead was the first event of its kind in the whole history of the universe. He is the "first fruits," the "pioneer of life." He has forced open a door that has been locked since the death of the first man. He has met, fought, and beaten the King of Death. Everything is different

*because He has done so. This is the beginning of the New
Creation: a new chapter in cosmic history has been opened.[1]*

Reflection Questions

- Would the cross be good news without the resurrection? Why or why not?

- Why is Jesus' bodily resurrection so important? What does this tell us about God's view of our physicality?

- If Jesus is the "first fruits" of resurrection, what does that mean for you?

- How does the hope of future resurrection change our perspective on life right now?

Prayer

Great God and Heavenly Father,

This is almost too good to be true: Jesus has defeated death itself! He is risen! He is alive! Thank you for this marvelous truth. Help me live today in the power of his resurrection. And when my dying day comes, help me face death with the confidence of knowing that on the last day, Christ will also raise up my mortal body in glory.

Amen.

---

1 C. S. Lewis, Miracles (New York, NY: HarperCollins, 1947) 236-237.

Day 11

The Triumph of the Cross

Since therefore the children share in flesh and
blood, he himself likewise partook of the same
things, that through death he might destroy the one
who has the power of death, that is, the devil, and
deliver all those who through fear of death were
subject to lifelong slavery.
(Hebrews 2:14–15)

SCRIPTURE DESCRIBES THE WORK OF CHRIST as the triumph over evil: his victory over Satan, sin, and death. John writes that "the reason the Son of God appeared was to destroy the works of the devil" (1 John 3:8). Paul says that in the cross, Jesus "disarmed the rulers and authorities and put them to open shame, by triumphing over them in him" (Col. 2:15). And in Hebrews we read that Christ became incarnate, "that through death he might destroy the one who has the power of death, that is, the devil, and deliver all those who through fear of death were subject to lifelong slavery" (Heb. 2:14–15).

In the death and resurrection of Christ, the decisive victory over sin, Satan, and death was won. Of course this raises a question: if this is so, why is there still so much evil and suffering in the world? Let me answer with a story.

There was an elderly widow who attended a little church I once pastored in Texas. Her name was Merleen, and though she was very kind, she was one of the toughest ladies I've ever met. She had grown up on the farm and could grow—or kill—anything! Merleen's utter fearlessness of rattlesnakes captured my interest. She had killed dozens of snakes, more than twenty in just one year! Merleen once found a rattlesnake on her farm, but didn't have a hoe nearby to kill it. She wasn't about to let it get away, so she dropped a boulder on the snake—not killing it, but pinning it to the ground. The decisive victory against the rattler was won then and there. Then she left to fetch her hoe and returned to take the snake's head off once and for all.

In the death of Christ, the decisive defeat of sin, Satan, death, and hell was won. Jesus crushed the serpent's head. Satan was disarmed and defeated, though not completely destroyed. He is like that rattlesnake pinned to the ground: still dangerous, still able to bite, but with far less authority. As Merleen returned to finish off the snake, so Jesus will return to establish his kingdom and defeat evil once and for all.

Reflection Questions

- Have you experienced the victory of Jesus over sin and evil in your life?
- Do you recognize that Satan is both a defeated foe and a dangerous enemy?
- How does the triumph of the cross over sin need to be expressed in your life today?

Prayer

Thank you, Father, for the victory of your Son over sin, Satan, death, and hell. Thank you that the devil is a defeated foe. Help me live today in the power of Christ's triumph. Defeat the power of sin in my life, for the sake of Jesus, my mighty King.

Amen.

Day 12

The Gift of the Holy Spirit

> "This Jesus God raised up, and of that we all are
> witnesses. Being therefore exalted at the right hand
> of God, and having received from the Father the
> promise of the Holy Spirit, he has poured out this
> that you yourselves are seeing and hearing."
> (Acts 2:32–33)

IN HIS RESURRECTION AND EXALTATION, Christ did far more than return to us our humanity. Even as the Son of Man departed from the earth, he sent us his Spirit. This was a pivotal event, unprecedented in the history of God's saving deeds. As Peter points out, it was also the fulfillment of Joel's prophecy that God would pour his Spirit out in the "last days" (Joel 2:28–32; Acts 2:17–21).

True, the Spirit of God was active before the coming of Christ. Scripture speaks of the Spirit's involvement in both creation (Gen. 1:2) and redemption (Isa. 63:7–14). From Peter and Paul, we know that the Spirit was also the agent of God's self-revelation through Scripture (2 Peter 1:21; 2 Tim. 3:14–17). But it is especially in the life and ministry of Jesus that we make our acquaintance with the Holy Spirit. "In the coming of Jesus, the Day of the Spirit had finally dawned."[1]

The Holy Spirit was intimately connected with Jesus throughout his entire life. Prior to Jesus' virginal conception an angel said to Mary, "the Holy Spirit will come upon you, and the power of the Most High will overshadow you" (Luke 1:35; *cf.* Matt. 1:18, 20). When Jesus was baptized by John the Baptist in the Jordan River, the Father anointed him with the Spirit (Matt. 3:16; Mark 1:10; Luke 3:22). Then Jesus was immediately driven into the wilderness by the Spirit for a

---

1 Sinclair B. Ferguson, *The Holy Spirit* (Downers Grove, IL: InterVarsity Press, 1996) 33.

season of testing (Matt. 4:1; Mark 1:12; Luke 4:1). Luke says that Jesus was "full of the Spirit" when this happened; he afterward returned to Galilee in "the power of the Spirit" (Luke 4:14).

In his death, Jesus offered himself as an atoning sacrifice through the Holy Spirit (Heb. 9:14). Paul tells us that Jesus was "declared to be the Son of God in power according to the Spirit of holiness by his resurrection from the dead" (Rom. 1:4). After Jesus' resurrection he breathed on his disciples, saying "receive the Holy Spirit" (John 20:22). Then followed Jesus' ascension and Pentecost, when the Spirit was poured out on the church, *as the Spirit of Christ.*

The exaltation of Christ inaugurated the new age of the Spirit. Jesus, the quintessential Spirit-filled one, the Last Adam, has lived and died in our place. He is now exalted in glorified humanity. In this exalted position, the Spirit so identifies with the risen Lord Jesus that Paul speaks of Christ as "life-giving Spirit" (1 Cor. 15:45) and the "Lord of the Spirit"[2] (2 Cor. 3:18). As Sinclair Ferguson writes,

> *From womb to tomb to throne, the Spirit was the constant companion of the Son. As a result, when he comes to Christians to indwell them, he comes as the Spirit of Christ in such a way that to possess him is to possess Christ himself, just as to lack him is to lack Christ.*[3]

This is important for us to grasp because *the Spirit, as given by our exalted Lord, is the agent who personally effects our transformation.* When we embrace Christ revealed in the gospel, he gives us his Spirit. The Holy Spirit remakes us after Christ's likeness, changing us by the sight of his glory into his very image (2 Cor. 3:18). We are dependent on the Spirit for every inch of progress in our pursuit of holiness and transformation.

---

2 On this rendering, see further notes on Day 13.
3 Ferguson, *The Holy Spirit,* 37.

Reflection Questions

- If you are a Christian, you have received the Holy Spirit (Rom. 8:9). But are you living in conscious dependence on the Spirit?

- Have you recognized your need for the ongoing ministry of the Spirit?

- Have you asked him to fill you and give you strength?

Prayer

Father,

I am weak and need your strength. I am helpless and need your power. Would you strengthen me today by the power of your Spirit? Help me to live in glad and grateful obedience to you, empowered by your own might. In Jesus' name.

Amen.

Day 13

The New Age of the Spirit

> And we all, with unveiled face, beholding the
> glory of the Lord, are being transformed into
> the same image from one degree of glory to
> another. For this comes from the Lord who is
> the Spirit.
>
> (2 Corinthians 3:18)

As we saw in the previous meditation, the exaltation of Jesus Christ inaugurated the new age of the Spirit. In his risen, exalted, and glorified human nature Christ has now bequeathed his Spirit to the church (see Acts 2). This is the first down payment of our inheritance and the effective guarantee of our salvation (Eph. 1:13-14).

This is crucial for us to grasp because *the Holy Spirit, as given by our exalted Lord, is the agent who personally effects our transformation.*

When we embrace Christ as revealed in the gospel, he gives us his Spirit. The Holy Spirit remakes us after Christ's likeness, changing us by the sight of his glory into his very image (2 Cor. 3:18). We are dependent on the Spirit for every inch of progress in our pursuit of holiness and transformation. As Calvin wrote,

> It is the Spirit that inflames our hearts with the fire of
> ardent love for God and for our neighbor. Every day he
> mortifies and every day consumes more and more of the
> vices of our evil desire or greed, so that, if there are some
> good deeds in us, these are the fruits and the virtues of
> his grace; and without the Spirit there is in us nothing but
> darkness of understanding and perversity of heart.[1]

---

1 John Calvin, *Instruction in Faith* (1537), Paul T. Fuhrmann, trans., (Louisville, KY: Westminster John Knox Press, 1977) 52.

This is the life-giving ministry of the Spirit in the new covenant (2 Cor. 3:4–4:6). Writing with rich biblical insight of how "the Spirit's task is to restore glory to a fallen creation," Ferguson continues:

> As Calvin well says, this world was made a theatre for God's glory. Throughout it he displays visibly the perfections of his invisible nature. Particularly in man and woman, his image, that glory was to be reflected. But they refused to glorify God (Rom. 1:21); they defiled the reflector (Rom. 1:28) and fell short of his glory (Rom. 3:23).
>
> But now, in Christ who is "the radiance of God's glory" (Heb. 1:2), that glory is restored. Having become flesh for us, he has now been exalted in our flesh yet in glory. The eschatological goal of creation has been consummated in him as its firstfruits. Now he sends his Spirit, the intimate companion of his entire incarnation, to recover glory in us. So it is that "we, who with unveiled faces reflect the Lord's glory, are being transformed into his likeness with ever-increasing glory, which comes from the Lord, who is the Spirit [or, the Lord of the Spirit]" (2 Cor. 3:18).
>
> The purpose for which the Spirit is given is, therefore, nothing less than the reproduction of the image of God, that is transformation into the likeness of Christ who is himself the image of God. To receive the Spirit is to be inaugurated into the effects of this ongoing ministry.[2]

Reflection Questions

- For what purpose has God given us his Spirit?
- How does knowing that the Holy Spirit is the Spirit *of Jesus* make a difference in your pursuit of Christlikeness?
- How can you express dependence on the Spirit today?

---

2 Ferguson, *The Holy Spirit*, 91-92.

Prayer

Spirit of the Exalted and Enthroned Son of God, fall fresh on me. Reproduce the character of Christ in me today. Write his image on my heart. Transform me to his likeness. Strengthen and fill me with your power, for Jesus' sake.

Amen

Day 14

Turning and Trusting

> ... I did not shrink from declaring to you anything
> that was profitable, and teaching you in public and
> from house to house, testifying both to Jews and to
> Greeks of repentance toward God and of faith in our
> Lord Jesus Christ.
> (Acts 20:20–21)

HOW DO WE RESPOND TO THE GOSPEL, this good news of Jesus
Christ, crucified, risen, and exalted? The answer is best expressed by
two words: turning and trusting. Or, in biblical language, repentance
and faith (Acts 20:21; Heb. 6:1).

To repent is to change one's mind and alter directions: to turn
around, to do an about-face. Perhaps the best illustration comes
from baseball. A Major League baseball pitcher like Yohan Santana
throws a 94 mph fast ball, or a 76 mph change-up (which looks
like a fast ball, but drops in speed by 18 mph), or an 87 mph slider,
straight through the center of the plate. Then, with a loud "crack,"
the ball meets the bat of a hard-hitting batter like Ryan Howard
(58 home runs in 2006!). Do you know what the ball does? It changes
direction. It repents! And when rebellious human beings encounter
the life-transforming power of God through the good news of Christ
crucified, risen, and exalted, they change direction.

Repentance always involves both turning *from* and turning *to*.
Scripture speaks of turning from idols (Acts 14:15, 1 Thess. 1:9),
turning from Satan (Acts 26:18), turning from sins (2 Chron. 6:26),
and turning from darkness (Acts 26:18). But repentance also means
turning to light (Acts 26:18) and to God himself (Hos. 14:2; Joel 2:19;
Amos 4:8; Acts 14:15; 15:19; 2 Cor. 3:16).

Repentance, furthermore, is not a onetime event, but a lifelong
process. As Martin Luther said in his *Ninety-five Theses,* "When our

Lord and Master, Jesus Christ, said 'Repent', He called for the entire life of believers to be one of penitence."[1]

The flip side of repentance is faith. Faith involves trusting in Jesus Christ and relying on him and all that he has accomplished for us. As the Westminster Confession of Faith states, "the principal acts of saving faith are accepting, receiving, and resting upon Christ alone for justification, sanctification, and eternal life."[2]

Repentance and faith involve not only turning from sin and trusting in Jesus to save us from our *unrighteousness*, but also turning from our "goodness" and trusting Jesus to save us from our *self-righteousness* (see Phil. 3:7–9).

Finally, we should always remember that faith and repentance belong together. Genuine faith is always a repentant faith. And true repentance is always a believing repentance. As Richard Lovelace writes, "Faith and repentance are not separable qualities. To have faith is to receive God's Word as truth and rest upon it in dependent trust; to repent is to have a new mind toward God, oneself, Christ, and the world, committing one's heart to new obedience to God."[3]

Isaac Watts beautifully expressed the heart of repentant faith in the lyrics of this hymn:

No more, my God, I boast no more
Of all the duties I have done;
I quit the hopes I held before,
To trust the merits of Thy Son

Now, for the loss I bear His name,
What was my gain I count my loss;
My former pride I call my shame,
And nail my glory to His cross.

---

1 Martin Luther, "The Ninety-Five Theses" in John Dillenberger, ed., *Martin Luther: Selections from His Writings* (New York, NY: Anchor Books, 1962) 490.

2 *Westminster Confession of Faith*, Chapter XIV.

3 Richard Lovelace, *Dynamics of Spiritual Life: An Evangelical Theology of Renewal* (Downers Grove, IL: Inter-Varsity Press, 1979) 102.

Yes, and I must and will esteem
All things but loss for Jesus' sake;
O may my soul be found in Him,
And of His righteousness partake!

The best obedience of my hands
Dares not appear before Thy throne;
But faith can answer Thy demands,
By pleading what my Lord has done.[4]

Reflection Questions

- How are faith and repentance related?

- Have you turned from sin and trusted in the all-sufficient work of the crucified, risen, and exalted Christ? He both commands and invites you to do so now (1 John 3:23; Matt. 11:28–30). This is the first crucial step toward genuine transformation.

Prayer

Father,

I have nothing to contribute to my salvation except my sin. My best obedience and my most sincere repentance are insufficient. My hands are absolutely empty. My one and only hope is Jesus, to whom I now turn and in whom I now trust. Please accept me for Jesus' sake.

Amen.

---

4 Isaac Watts, "No More My God," n.d.

Day 15

Justified by Faith Alone

Therefore, since we have been justified by faith, we
have peace with God through our Lord Jesus Christ.
(Romans 5:1)

WHEN WE LOOK CLOSELY at what Christ did for us on the cross, we realize that he represented us in two ways. First, he represented us by taking the punishment of our sins—past, present, and future. "For our sake he made him to be sin who knew no sin" (2 Cor. 5:21a). "For Christ also suffered once for sins, the righteous for the unrighteous" (1 Peter 3:18a). And second, he represented us in his perfect obedience and righteousness. "By the one man's obedience the many will be made righteous" (Rom. 5:19b).

This double representation clarifies how we can be justified before God. We all begin with a twofold need. We need to have our violations of God's law, our sins, paid in full. And we need a perfect record of obedient righteousness by which to enter God's eternal kingdom and presence. Jesus has secured both of these benefits for us. He paid the penalty for our sins, and he lived a perfectly righteous life on our behalf.

On the cross, God treated Jesus as if he had lived my sinful life, so that he could then treat me as if I had lived the perfect, obedient life of Jesus. The only way I can be accepted as righteous by God is through the doing and dying of Jesus on my behalf. He died the death I should have died and lived the life I should have lived. God counted Jesus as a sinner so he could count me as righteous. The Father accepts me, not because of anything I have done or can do, not even because of anything he has done *in* me, but solely because of what Jesus Christ has done *for* me. His flawless record is counted as mine. As Paul says, "For our sake he made him to be sin who knew no sin, so that in him we might become the righteousness of God" (2 Cor. 5:21).

So, how do we benefit from this grace?

We receive justification from God by faith alone. "For we hold that one is justified by faith apart from works of the law" (Rom. 3:28). "Therefore, since we have been justified by faith, we have peace with God through our Lord Jesus Christ" (Rom. 5:1). Faith is believing in and relying upon God. It is "not a work, but a relinquishment of all work, an unqualified trust in God who gives life to the dead (4:17), who raised Christ from the dead (4:24), who in Christ gave 'a righteousness from God.'"[1]

Justification is by grace alone, through faith alone, in Christ alone. God accepts us as righteous not because of anything we do, and not even because of anything he has done *in us*, but solely because of what Jesus Christ has done *for us*.

Reflection Questions

- When you struggle with guilt over your failures as a Christian, what do you do?
- Do you ever try to pay God back by working harder or doing better? Why is this an insufficient motive for obedience?
- Does understanding that Christ not only paid for your sins, but also obeyed in your place, deepen your gratitude and love for him?

Prayer

Father,

Thank you that Christ is my sacrifice, my sin-bearer, my obedience, my righteousness, my everything. Nothing I could ever do or say could pay back the debt I owe. I am saved by grace alone, through faith alone, in Christ alone. Thank you for this indescribable gift! Let my obedience to you flow from the gratitude that fills my heart when I remember this wonderful grace.

In Jesus' name,

Amen.

---

1 Herman Bavinck, with the Greek words omitted, in Herman Bavinck, John Bolt, gen. ed., John Vriend, trans., *Reformed Dogmatics: Volume 4: Holy Spirit, Church, and New Creation* (Grand Rapids, MI: Baker Academic, 2008) 211.

Day 16

The Basis of Our Acceptance

*Therefore, since we have been justified by faith, we
have peace with God through our Lord Jesus Christ.*
(Romans 5:1)

ALL TOO OFTEN, RELIGIOUS PEOPLE view their acts of piety or
moral efforts as a means of gaining acceptance with God. Check
yourself now. Even if you've been a Christian for a long time, don't
you sometimes feel like God is more pleased with you on days when
you've been faithful in daily devotions than those rushed days when
you neglected time in the Word and prayer? Do you tend to view
your relationship with God as a long list of "dos and don'ts"? Is your
obedience to God motivated by love and characterized by joy—
or guilt and fear? Is it easy for you to admit your failures and take
ownership of your sins? Or does the possibility of being exposed feel
threatening to your sense of well-being?

As in Luther's case, our relationship with God can easily become
based on our own performance, rather than the performance of
Christ. Even good spiritual disciplines, such as Bible reading, prayer,
and worship, become, in our minds, like rungs on the ladder to
heaven. We may not express it this way. In fact, we might even deny
it. But functionally, and practically, we live as if approval from God
depended upon our obedience, instead of Christ's obedience for us.

As Richard Lovelace wisely writes:

*Only a fraction of the present body of professing Christians
are solidly appropriating the justifying work of Christ
in their lives. Many have so slight an apprehension of
God's holiness and of the extent and guilt of their sin that
consciously they see little need for justification, although
below the surface their lives are deeply guilt-ridden and*

*insecure. Many others have a theoretical commitment to
this doctrine, but in their day-to-day existence they rely
on their sanctification for justification . . . drawing their
assurance of acceptance with God from their sincerity,
their past experience of conversion, their recent religious
performance or the relative infrequency of their conscious,
willful disobedience. Few enough know to start each day
with a thoroughgoing stand upon Luther's platform: you
are accepted, looking outward in faith and claiming the
wholly alien righteousness of Christ as the only ground
for acceptance, relaxing in that quality of trust which will
produce increasing sanctification as faith is active in love
and gratitude.*[1]

Not only do I agree with Lovelace's assessment, but I think this
uncovers one of the fundamental mistakes we make in our thinking
about spiritual formation. Sometimes believers fall into a performance
trap. We think that our obedience—our degree of cooperation with
God's ongoing work of transformation—is the *basis*, rather than the
result, of our acceptance with God.

Reflection Questions

- Work through the questions in the first paragraph of today's
  reading. Do you find that your sense of God's acceptance is
  determined by your performance? Why is this wrong?

- How do you think your life would change if you followed
  Lovelace's advice and began each and every day "with
  a thoroughgoing stand upon Luther's platform: *you are
  accepted*, looking outward in faith and claiming the
  wholly alien righteousness of Christ as the only ground
  for acceptance"?

---

1 Lovelace, *Dynamics of Spiritual Life*, 101.

Prayer

Father,

The gospel tells me that the verdict is in: Not guilty! Help me to believe with all my heart that this too-good-to-be-true news really is true. I am already accepted and nothing I can do can alter my acceptance in Christ. Teach me to live daily in this strength and assurance of this reality.

In Jesus' name,

Amen.

Day 17

Law or Gospel?

> There is therefore now no condemnation for those
> who are in Christ Jesus. For the law of the Spirit of life
> has set you free in Christ Jesus from the law of sin and
> death. For God has done what the law, weakened by
> the flesh, could not do. By sending his own Son in the
> likeness of sinful flesh and for sin, he condemned sin in
> the flesh, in order that the righteous requirement of the
> law might be fulfilled in us, who walk not according to
> the flesh but according to the Spirit.
>
> (Romans 8:1–4)

AS BELIEVERS WE WANT TO BE HOLY, but sometimes we pursue holiness as if it were *for* grace—a condition for being welcomed by God, rather than *from* grace—an overflow of our love for the Father who freely welcomes us through Christ and his cross.

This is not only a misunderstanding, but a hindrance to our growth in Christ. To trust in our holiness as the ground of our acceptance with God is *legalism*. Legalism takes the law, rather than grace, as its starting point. Legalism is law based and performance oriented. Grasping the significance of justification protects us from this error.

This is not to say that the law is bad. Paul defended the essential goodness and holiness of the law (Rom. 7:7–12). But though the law is good, it is not able to save. As Luther himself later wrote:

> *The law is divine and holy. Let the law have his glory, but*
> *yet no law, be it never so divine and holy, ought to teach me*
> *that I am justified, and shall live through it. I grant it may*
> *teach me that I ought to love God and my neighbour; also*
> *to live in chastity, soberness, patience, etc., but it ought not*

to show me, how I should be delivered from sin, the devil, death, and hell. Here I must take counsel of the Gospel. I must hearken to the Gospel, which teacheth me, not what I ought to do, (for that is the proper office of the law,) but what Jesus Christ the Son of God hath done for me: to wit, that He suffered and died to deliver me from sin and death. The gospel willeth me to receive this, and to believe it. And this is the truth of the Gospel. It is also the principal article of all Christian doctrine, wherein the knowledge of all godliness consisteth. Most necessary it is, therefore, that we should know this article well, teach it unto others, and beat it into their heads continually.[1]

All knowledge of godliness consists in this—knowing and embracing the truth of the gospel, that I am accepted by God not because of what I do, but because of what Christ has done for me. Until the sin-removing, curse-canceling power of Christ's death is understood and embraced, we will make no true progress in actually conquering sin and growing in grace. John Owen said, "There is no death of sin without the death of Christ."[2] The penalty of sin must be removed before the power of sin can be broken. But Scripture tells us that the penalty—the curse of the law—is removed! "Christ redeemed us from the curse of the law by becoming a curse for us—for it is written, 'Cursed is everyone who is hanged on a tree'" (Gal. 3:13).

Isn't this the greatest news in the world? The verdict of God's final judgment on the believer is given the moment he or she trusts in Christ—*Not Guilty!* "There is therefore *now* no condemnation for those who are in Christ Jesus" (Rom. 8:1, emphasis added). "Who shall bring any charge against God's elect? It is God who justifies. Who is to condemn? Christ Jesus is the one who died—more than that, who was raised—who is at the right hand of God, who indeed is interceding for us" (Rom. 8:33–34). Justice is satisfied in the death

---

1 Martin Luther, *A Commentary on St. Paul's Epistle to the Galatians* (London: James Clarke & Co., 1953) 101.

2 John Owen, *Of the Mortification of Sin in Believers* in William H. Gould, ed., *The Works of John Owen*, vol. 6, (Carlisle, PA: The Banner of Truth Trust, 1967 reprint of 1850-53 edition) 33.

of Christ for sinners! We rejoice in this confidence: "If we confess our sins, he is faithful and *just* to forgive us our sins and to cleanse us from all unrighteousness" (1 John 1:9, emphasis added). Notice it is not only the faithfulness of God that assures us of pardon, but his *justice!* The debt of our sin was paid on the cross, and that payment is sufficient. God requires no further payment from us. *That* is divine justice.

> *If Thou hast my discharge procured,*
> *And freely in my room endured*
> *The whole of wrath divine:*
> *Payment God cannot twice demand,*
> *First at my bleeding Surety's hand,*
> *And then again at mine.*[3]

Therefore, we do not pursue personal transformation *for* grace, which would be legalism, but *from* grace. We live holy lives not in order to get ourselves right with God, but because he has already set us right in Jesus Christ. Justification precedes, and is the necessary basis of, actual transformation.

Reflection Questions

- What is legalism? Do you see any evidence of legalism in your life?

- What, according to Martin Luther, is the difference between the law and the gospel? What does the law show us? What does the gospel show us?

- What are some practical things you could do to "beat the gospel into your head continually"?

---

3 Augustus Toplady, "From Whence This Fear and Unbelief," 1772.

Prayer

Thank you, gracious Father, that my debt is paid in full, that your justice is fully satisfied with the death of Christ for my sins, and, even more, that your justice now demands the forgiveness of my sins. Beat this truth into my head. Seal it to my heart. And help me live a holy life in grateful response to the grace you have already given to me in Jesus.

Amen.

Day 18

Slaves or Sons?

> But when the fullness of time had come, God sent forth
> his Son, born of woman, born under the law, to redeem
> those who were under the law, so that we might receive
> adoption as sons. And because you are sons, God has
> sent the Spirit of his Son into our hearts, crying, "Abba!
> Father!" So you are no longer a slave, but a son, and if a
> son, then an heir through God.
>
> (Galatians 4:4–7)

THE DOCTRINE OF JUSTIFICATION transforms the nature of our
obedience. We relate to God not as slaves, fearing the condemnation
of an angry master, but as sons, confident in the love and acceptance
of our Father.

This was the truth that changed Martin Luther's life. And two
hundred years later, it changed the life of John Wesley. John Stott
describes Wesley's post-graduate Oxford days when he a member of
a small religious group called the Holy Club:

> *He was the son of a clergyman and already a clergyman
> himself. He was orthodox in belief, religious in practice,
> upright in his conduct and full of good works. He and his
> friends visited the inmates of the prisons and work-houses
> of Oxford. They took pity on the slum children of the city,
> providing them with food, clothing, and education. They
> observed Saturday as the Sabbath as well as Sunday. They
> went to church and to Holy Communion. They gave alms,
> searched the Scriptures, fasted and prayed. But they were
> bound in the fetters of their own religion, for they were
> trusting in themselves that they were righteous instead of
> putting their trust in Jesus Christ and in Him crucified.*

A few years later, John Wesley (in his own words) came to "trust in Christ, in Christ only for salvation" and was given an inward assurance that his sins had been taken away. After this, looking back to his pre-conversion experience, he wrote: "I had even then the faith of a servant, though not that of a son."[1]

There's the difference! Like Luther and Wesley, many people relate to God on the basis of duty and works, rather than sonship and grace. They trust in themselves, rather than Christ. But when we grasp that our acceptance with God is based on his grace given to us in Christ alone, the motivational center of gravity in our spirituality shifts. Now we are propelled not by guilt, but grace. We relate to him not as servants, but as sons.[2]

To see the law by Christ fulfilled
To hear his pardoning voice
Changes a slave into a child
And duty to choice.[3]

Do you realize the kind of confidence this wonderful truth can build into your relationship with God? My heart brims with joy and my eyes fill with tears when I reflect on God's gracious work for me in Christ. He has canceled the curse my sins deserved! Justice is satisfied and I am pardoned, accepted as righteous before the judge's—*my Father's*—throne. The assurance of forgiveness granted to us through the cross is irrevocably life changing.

Does the realization of what God has done for you in Christ cause your heart to burst with joy? Do you know with glad certainty that your sins are forgiven, that you stand before the throne of God

---

1 John R. W. Stott, *The Message of Galatians* (Downers Grove, IL: InterVarsity Press, 1984) 109.
2 By keeping the term "sons" (as opposed to the more gender-neutral "children" or "sons and daughters") I do not mean to infer any inferiority in a female's status with God. The terminology, rather, reflects the cultural norms of the first century, when the New Testament was written, when sons had unique rights as heirs.
3 William Cowper, Kevin Twit, "Love Constraining to Obedience," © 1988 Kevin Twit Music.

robed in the flawless obedience and perfection of Jesus? When we grasp, or rather are grasped by, this grace, our whole approach to personal change is radically altered. We no longer pursue holiness to alleviate our guilt. Rather, we serve our Father with the freedom of children who delight to bear his likeness.

> *Mercy speaks by Jesus' blood;*
> *Hear and sing, ye sons of God;*
> *Justice satisfied indeed;*
> *Christ has full atonement made.*[4]

Reflection Questions

- Do you primarily view God as Father or Judge? Is your obedience to God that of a slave or a child?
- Reflect for a few moments on today's reading from Galatians 4. How should the gifts of God's Son and God's Spirit change the way you relate to God?

Prayer

Heavenly Father,

Thank you for your two greatest gifts: the gift of your Son to secure my redemption and the gift of your Spirit to seal my adoption. Thank you for making me your child. Help me now trust you as Father and live in the joyful and holy freedom that belongs to your children.

In Jesus' name,

Amen.

---

4 William Gadsby, Derek Webb, Sandra McCracken, "Mercy Speaks by Jesus' Blood." © 2002 Niphon Music (ASCAP) / Same Old Dress Music, Inc. (ASCAP).

Day 19

Changing the Heart

> For no good tree bears bad fruit, nor again does a
> bad tree bear good fruit, for each tree is known by
> its own fruit. For figs are not gathered from thorn
> bushes, nor are grapes picked from a bramble bush.
> The good person out of the good treasure of his
> heart produces good, and the evil person out of his
> evil treasure produces evil, for out of the abundance
> of the heart his mouth speaks.
> (Luke 6:43–45)

THE HEART IS THE ESSENTIAL "YOU." "As in water, face reflects face, so the heart of man reflects the man" (Prov. 27:19). You are what your heart is. This is why Scripture says, "man looks on the outward appearance, but the LORD looks on the heart" (1 Sam. 16:7). Therefore, to change *you*, your *heart* must change. Paul David Tripp's unpacking of this is classic:

> Let's say I have an apple tree in my backyard. Each year its apples are dry, wrinkled, brown, and pulpy. After several seasons my wife says, 'It doesn't make any sense to have this huge tree and never be able to eat any apples. Can't you do something?' One day my wife looks out the window to see me in the yard, carrying branch cutters, an industrial grade staple gun, a ladder, and two bushels of apples.
>
> I climb the ladder, cut off all the pulpy apples, and staple shiny, red apples onto every branch of the tree. From a distance our tree looks like it is full of a beautiful harvest. But if you were my wife, what would you be thinking of me at this moment?

*If a tree produces bad apples year after year, there is
something drastically wrong with its system, down to its
very roots. I won't solve the problem by stapling new apples
onto the branches. They also will rot because they are not
attached to a life-giving root system. And next spring, I will
have the same problem again. I will not see a new crop of
healthy apples because my solution has not gone to the
heart of the problem. If the tree's roots remain unchanged,
it will never produce good apples.*

*The point is . . . much of what we do to produce growth
and change in ourselves and others is little more than "fruit
stapling." It attempts to exchange apples for apples without
examining the heart, the root behind the behavior. This is
the very thing for which Christ criticized the Pharisees.
Change that ignores the heart will seldom transform the life.
For a while, it may seem like the real thing, but it will prove
temporary and cosmetic.*[1]

All too often, strategies for pursuing holiness center on fruit-stapling instead of deep heart transformation. We try to live by lists: elaborate codes for moral behavior that tell us exactly what to do and don't do. Realizing the insufficiency of this approach, how do we actually get to the heart of sin?

We will never get to the heart of sinful behavior until we uncover the underlying desires of the heart that motivate us. Let me illustrate. A few years ago, while planning for a mission trip to South Africa, I experienced an exaggerated amount of anxiety and stress. A friend had found the tickets for us and told me we would fly from South Bend to Chicago to New York, and then from New York to Johannesburg, South Africa. It was good deal, so I bought the tickets. Only two weeks later did I realize that we would be flying *in* from Chicago to the La Guardia airport in New York, but *out* to Johannesburg from JFK! We would only have a short length of time to pick up our luggage, be transported to JFK, and check in for our

1 Paul David Tripp, *Instruments in the Redeemer's Hands: People in Need of Change Helping People in Need of Change* (Phillipsburg, NJ: P & R Publishing, 2002) 63.

international flight. My anxiety skyrocketed! You might think that the reason for this sinful worry was an underlying desire for control. But that wasn't it at all. I wasn't stressed about missing a flight. The truth is, I could care less about the inconvenience. My anxiety was rooted in my fear of losing respect from the team members who were accompanying me. I was afraid of losing face. My sin was rooted in a desire: the desire for approval.

You and I will never make genuine progress in spiritual transformation until we address the idolatrous desires that lie at the root of our sinful behaviors. This means that when we're diagnosing our problems with sin, we have to plow deep to unearth the drives, motives, intentions and inclinations of the heart. We have to search out, with God's help and sometimes the help of others, the longings and cravings, the hopes and dreams, the pleasures and fears that drive us. Only when these are powerfully transformed by grace, will we really change.

Reflection Questions

- Think about one of your ongoing sin struggles. Have you been trying to change by addressing behaviors only? Or have you addressed the deeper motives of your heart?

- Are your attempts to change more focused on "fruit stapling" than real inward change?

- What are your deepest desires? Have these desires in any way replaced your desire to glorify God? Ask God to change your heart.

Prayer

Father,

Change my heart. Change my motives, ambitions, fears, delights, and desires. Help me to see that my greatest joy will be found in glorifying and obeying you.

In Jesus' name,

Amen.

Day 20

Regeneration

> But when the goodness and loving kindness of God
> our Savior appeared, he saved us, not because of
> works done by us in righteousness, but according to
> his own mercy, by the washing of regeneration and
> renewal of the Holy Spirit, whom he poured out on
> us richly through Jesus Christ our Savior, so that
> being justified by his grace we might become heirs
> according to the hope of eternal life.
>
> (Titus 3:4–7)

CHRISTIANITY IS NOT SIMPLY A MATTER of making right decisions or changing our behavior by willpower. There must be something deeper, more radical. We need heart transplants. The affections God demands can only arise from hearts made new, transformed by his grace. This is what God demands. This is what God promises to give.

In Deuteronomy, God commands his people to seek, love, serve, obey, and turn to him with all their hearts (Deut. 4:29, 6:5, 10:12, 11:13, 13:3, 26:16, 30:2, 10). But knowing the inability of his people to do this, he also commands them to circumcise their hearts, turning away from stubbornness (Deut. 10:16). Then, after prophesying Israel's eventual disobedience to the terms of God's covenant with them, God promises to gather them to himself again, and change their hearts.

> And the LORD your God will circumcise your heart and the
> heart of your offspring, so that you will love the LORD your God
> with all your heart and with all your soul, that you may live.
>
> (Deut. 30:6)

God promises to do *for* them what he has demanded *of* them. This promise foreshadows the promises of the new covenant that appear later in Jeremiah and Ezekiel.

I will make with them an everlasting covenant, that I will not turn away from doing good to them. And I will put the fear of me in their hearts, that they may not turn from me.

(Jer. 32:40)

I will sprinkle clean water on you, and you shall be clean from all your uncleannesses, and from all your idols I will cleanse you. And I will give you a new heart, and a new spirit I will put within you. And I will remove the heart of stone from your flesh and give you a heart of flesh. And I will put my Spirit within you, and cause you to walk in my statutes and be careful to obey my rules.

(Ezek. 36:25–27)

In several places the New Testament refers to the new covenant, circumcision of the heart, and spiritual cleansing. Jesus is called the "mediator of the new covenant" (Heb. 9:15, 12:24; *cf.* Heb. 8:1–13) and in the Passover meal with his disciples the night before his death he said, "This cup that is poured out for you is the new covenant in my blood" (Luke 22:20). Paul calls himself a "minister of the new covenant" (2 Cor. 3:6), explaining his ministry as the life-giving, veil-removing ministry of the Spirit that opens the eyes to behold the transforming glory of Christ in the gospel (2 Cor. 3:1–4:6). Three times he references the inward circumcision of the heart from Deuteronomy 30:6, calling it "circumcision . . . of the heart, by the Spirit" (Rom. 2:28), the "real circumcision" (Phil. 3:3), and "a circumcision made without hands" that is accomplished "by putting off the body of the flesh, by the circumcision of Christ" (Col. 2:11), that is, through union with Christ in his burial and resurrection (Col. 2:12).

Jesus' familiar words to Nicodemus about being born "from above" (John 3:3) and born "of water and the Spirit" (v. 5) refer to the new covenant promise of spiritual cleansing from Ezekiel 36:25–27.

Paul weaves the same concepts into his explanation of salvation in Titus 3:4–7 (see above).

These passages demonstrate the depth of transformation we need and that God graciously provides for us through Jesus Christ. We need more than moral reformation and behavioral modification. We need inner cleansing, spiritual renewal, and new hearts—and God does that for us!

Though the full renovation of our hearts is an ongoing, lifelong process, God begins this work in the once-and-for-all, definitive event of new birth, or regeneration.[1] Regeneration, which Richard Lovelace calls "the beachhead of sanctification in the soul"[2] is God's mysterious work of imparting new life to the soul. Scripture uses many metaphors to describe this work of God, including birth (John 3:1–8; 1 Peter 1:3, 23), creation (2 Cor. 5:17; Eph. 2:10, 4:24), and resurrection (John 5:21; Eph. 2:1–7; Col. 2:12). Each of these metaphors reminds us that regeneration is not something we can do for ourselves, but something God has to do for us. We can no more regenerate ourselves than a baby can conceive itself, a world create itself, or a corpse raise itself to life. As John Piper writes, "God is the great Doer in this miracle of regeneration."[3]

These metaphors also teach us that regeneration produces change. It is the creation of light in our hearts (2 Cor. 4:6), being born again to a living hope (1 Peter 1:3), the infusion of new life to those who were spiritually dead (Eph. 2:5), resulting in the practice

---

1 David Peterson's comments on the relationship between sanctification and regeneration are helpful: "Regeneration involves a new birth to faith, hope and love, made possible by the Holy Spirit. Sanctification has to do with the new status and orientation of those who belong to God and to one another as his people. Sanctification means having a new identity, with the obligation to live according to that identity. Regeneration, which is a definitive, life-transforming work of the Spirit at the beginning of the Christian life, has its continuation in the process of renewal (cf. Eph. 4:22-24; Col. 3:9-11; Tit. 3:5-6). Sanctification has its continuation or extension in the life of holiness which the Spirit makes possible through faith in Christ." David Peterson, *Possessed by God: A New Testament Theology of Sanctification and Holiness* (Downers Grove, IL: InterVarsity Press, 1995) 63-64.

2 Richard F. Lovelace, *Dynamics of Spiritual Life: An Evangelical Theology of Renewal* (Downers Grove, IL: Inter-Varsity Press, 1979) 104.

3 John Piper, *Finally Alive: What Happens When We Are Born Again* (Ross-shire, Scotland: Christian Focus Publications, 2009) 22.

of righteousness, a love for others, and a faith in Christ which overcomes the world (1 John 2:29, 3:9, 4:7, 5:1, 4, 18).

No one has described this more beautifully than Charles Wesley in his lyrical description of the experience of new birth in his well-known hymn "And Can it Be":

> *Long my imprisoned spirit lay*
> *Fast bound in sin and nature's night*
> *Thine eye diffused a quickening ray*
> *I woke, the dungeon flamed with light*
> *My chains fell off, my heart was free*
> *I rose went forth and followed thee!*[4]

This is the beginning of God's glorious work in us. He takes our stony hearts, monstrous and deformed by sin as they are, and replaces them with new hearts. He cleanses us from idols by his Word, sanctifies and indwells us by his Spirit, creates us anew in Christ Jesus, grants us the gifts of repentance and faith, and renews the image of God within us. God gives what he demands.

Reflection Questions

- Why is regeneration necessary?
- What are some of the metaphors Scripture uses to describe regeneration? What do these word pictures teach us?
- Read through the passages in 1 John that describe the evidences of being "born of God" (1 John 2:29, 3:9, 4:7, 5:1, 4, 18). Do you see these evidences in your own life?

---

4 Charles Wesley, "And Can it Be" 1738.

Prayer

Father,

I cannot change my heart. I cannot change myself. I'm completely dependent on your grace. Thank you that through the work of your Spirit you have given me a new heart. Thank you for the gift of new birth. Help me now live in the faith, hope, and love that characterize your children.

In Jesus' name,

Amen.

Day 21
The Gospel Mystery of Sanctification

> What shall we say then? Are we to continue in sin
> that grace may abound? By no means! How can we
> who died to sin still live in it? Do you not know
> that all of us who have been baptized into Christ
> Jesus were baptized into his death? We were buried
> therefore with him by baptism into death, in order
> that, just as Christ was raised from the dead by the
> glory of the Father, we too might walk in newness of
> life. For if we have been united with him in a death
> like his, we shall certainly be united with him in
> a resurrection like his. We know that our old self
> was crucified with him in order that the body of sin
> might be brought to nothing, so that we would no
> longer be enslaved to sin. For one who has died has
> been set free from sin. Now if we have died with
> Christ, we believe that we will also live with him.
> We know that Christ, being raised from the dead,
> will never die again; death no longer has dominion
> over him. For the death he died he died to sin, once
> for all, but the life he lives he lives to God. So you
> also must consider yourselves dead to sin and alive
> to God in Christ Jesus.
> (Romans 6:1–11)

AS YOU READ THROUGH THESE VERSES from Romans 6, notice how
Paul connects our story to the gospel story. We were baptized into
his death and raised to walk in newness of life (vv. 3–4). His death
counts as ours, and since he died to sin (v. 10), the sway of sin in
our lives has been broken (vv. 6–7). The power of his resurrection
gives us life, both now and in the future (vv. 4–5, 8). The pattern

of the gospel—the death and resurrection of Christ—determines the pattern of our lives. This is what the seventeenth-century English Puritan Walter Marshall called "The Gospel Mystery of Sanctification."[1]

All our progress in actual change depends on this new relationship to Christ. He is in us and we are in him. In Christ, we have died to sin and are now alive to righteousness (v. 11).

This truth permeates the New Testament. Ephesians describes how we have been made alive, raised, and seated with Christ (Eph. 2:5–6). In Galatians, Paul says, "I have been crucified with Christ. It is no longer I who live, but Christ who lives in me. And the life I now live in the flesh I live by faith in the Son of God, who loved me and gave himself for me" (Gal. 2:19b–20). In language similar to Romans 6, Colossians says we have "been buried with [Christ] in baptism" and "raised with him through faith in the powerful working of God, who raised him from the dead" (Col. 2:12). Paul then shows how dying and rising with Christ determines our thinking and actions (Col. 3:1ff).

Through union with Christ, you are righteous (having been justified), new (regenerated), and holy (definitively sanctified). In this unbreakable union with Christ we are given a new history, a new identity, and a new destiny.

- We are given a new *history*, because his past counts as our past: his perfect life and obedient death are credited as ours. His death to the ruling power of sin counts as ours, securing our freedom from sin's tyranny.

- We are given a new *identity*, because when we are joined to Christ, God sees us in his Son. In fact, we become saints, children of God, and heirs with Christ.

---

1 Walter Marshall, *The Gospel Mystery of Sanctification: Growing in Holiness by Living in Union with Christ. A New Version Put Into Modern English by Bruce H. McRae* (Eugene, OR: Wipf & Stock Publishers, 2005). At the heart of Marshall's book is the doctrine of our union with Christ and the necessary implications of union with Christ for sanctification. "This is the key error Christians fall into in their lives: they think that even though they have been justified by a righteousness produced totally by Christ, they must be sanctified by a holiness produced totally by themselves" (39-40).

- We are given a new *destiny*, because in the resurrection
  of Christ, the age to come has dawned. His resurrection
  guarantees that we will be raised from the dead as well, and,
  in fact, empowers us to live in newness of life in the here
  and now.

Jesus has not just given us a ticket to heaven. He has changed
our essential identity. He has irrevocably altered the effect of our past
on our present and future by causing his death and resurrection to
count as ours. We really are new creatures, even as we press on by
God's grace to become more holy.

The point is that sanctification (freedom from the *dominion* of
sin), no less than justification (freedom from the *guilt* of sin), comes
through faith in Christ alone. *Everything* we need for life and godliness
is found in him! Transformation can happen in no other way.

The gospel reminds us that Christ himself is the one and only
human being who has perfectly imaged the holy character of God.
He is the pioneer of our salvation, the new Adam, and, therefore, the
head of the new creation. We can only reflect the image of God as
we become like Christ. And we can only become like him if we are
in him.

Reflection Questions

- Remember the old spiritual, "Were you there when they
  crucified my Lord?" What do you think Paul's answer to that
  question would be?

- Take a few moments to read the first two chapters of
  Ephesians. Circle every time you read the words "in (or with)
  Christ" or "in (or with) him." Write down what you learn.

Prayer

What grace, that I the chief of sinners, should be "found in Christ, not having a righteousness of my own that comes from the law, but that which comes through faith in Christ, the righteousness from God that depends on faith" (Philippians 3:9). Help me, gracious Father, to grasp the reality of my new identity in Christ and help me to become more and more like him as a result.

In Jesus' name,

Amen.

Day 22

Do Not Let Sin Reign

Let not sin therefore reign in your mortal body,
to make you obey its passions.
(Romans 6:12)

SINCE WE ARE DEAD TO SIN AND ALIVE TO GOD in Christ Jesus (v. 11), *we must not allow sin to control our actions.* "Let not sin therefore reign in your mortal bodies, to make you obey their passions" (v. 12). This command injects a dose of reality into our thinking. Though the old self is crucified, this doesn't mean the battle with sin is over. Sin still wages war against your soul, assaulting your thoughts and senses with passions demanding acquiescence. The old slave master still insists on your obedience! But you mustn't let sin rule.

This exhortation raises an important question: Does the believer still have a sinful nature? The answer depends on how "sinful nature" is defined. It is clear that the believer still contends against the flesh. "The desires of the flesh are against the Spirit, and the desires of the Spirit are against the flesh, for these are opposed to each other, to keep you from doing the things you want to do" (Gal. 5:17). So we still contend with sinful desires. I think this is also what Paul means in Romans 7, when he says, "I find it to be a law that when I want to do right, evil lies close at hand. For I delight in the law of God, in my inner being, but I see in my members another law waging war against the law of my mind and making me captive to the law of sin that dwells in my members" (Rom. 7:21–23). On a similar note, Peter exhorts us to "abstain from the passions of the flesh, which wage war against your soul" (1 Peter 2:11). So, yes—the believer still struggles against the sinful inclinations, passions, and the desires of the flesh.

Some teachers, however, view the flesh (or "old" or "sinful" nature) as a static, unchanging principle within the believer that constantly struggles against the Spirit (or "new" or "regenerate" nature) for control in a believer's life. The flesh and the new nature are like a pair of junkyard dogs (a black dog vs. a white dog, as the illustration usually goes) locked in a fierce, lifelong battle. Whichever one you feed wins. From this perspective, the Christian is something of a Jekyll and Hyde, a conflicted being with two personalities vying for mastery in his heart. Living in holiness depends on constantly counteracting the "old nature" with the power of the Spirit. As long as the believer is filled with the Spirit, the power of sin is counteracted— and the Christian can live a "victorious" (or "higher" or "deeper") life, *completely* free from all conscious and willful sin. On the other hand, believers who continue to struggle with sin are living in "defeat" because they pursue holiness in "the energy of the flesh," rather than abiding in Christ and being filled with the Spirit.

But this teaching fails in two ways. First, it fails to grasp the extensive scope of transformation that results from union with Christ. Implicit to this view of sanctification is the possibility that a true believer could live in habitual dominion to sin. But that would deny the radical change experienced by all who are joined to Christ.[1] As we learned earlier in this chapter, all believers are united to Christ in his death and resurrection. The black dog (or, to revert to theological language, "the old man") is dead! Therefore all believers are freed from sin's slavery and walk in newness of life. But, second, this teaching also fails to recognize that even mature and "spiritual" believers will continue to fight against sin throughout their lives. On one hand, we claim too little if we assert that believers can live in unbroken bondage to habitual sin. But on the other hand, we claim too much if we think we have achieved the kind of victory that removes us from the arena of struggle.

The truth is that though all believers will continue to contend with the remnants of indwelling sin, sin is not a power equal in influence to the Holy Spirit. Genuine and sustainable change is not only possible, but guaranteed by God's grace. A Christian's inner nature

---

1 This view also misunderstands the nature of sin, viewing it in terms of intentional actions, while neglecting to address sin on the motivational level. The victory over sin promised (and sometimes claimed) produces superficial triumphalism, at best. Worse, it may lead to naïve self-righteousness that is lacking in the self-awareness Paul demonstrated by calling himself the foremost of sinners (1 Tim. 1:15).

and personal identity as a human being have been fundamentally altered. We are no longer slaves of sin! The passions of sin do not reflect who we are in Christ. As 2 Corinthians 5:17 says, "If anyone is in Christ, he is a new creation. The old has passed away; behold, the new has come"!

But to live in line with your new identity, you must say, "No!" to the passions of sin. "For the grace of God has appeared, bringing salvation for all people, training us to *renounce* ungodliness and worldly passions, and to live self-controlled, upright, and godly lives in the present age" (Titus 2:11–12, my emphasis). Sin still dwells within—but it has no authority to master you. Don't let it control you!

Reflection Questions

- If we really are dead to sin through our union with Christ, why do we still experience conflict with sin?

- What two truths does much "victorious life" teaching fail to recognize?

- Paul says we must let not sin reign (Rom. 6:12) and must renounce ungodliness and worldly passions (Titus 2:11–12). Peter says we must abstain from the passions of the flesh (1 Peter 2:11). In other words, we must say no to sin. What sins do you need to say no to right now?

Prayer

Lord Jesus,

Thank you for breaking the power of canceled sin and setting me free. Enable me to recognize that, though sin still dwells within me, it has no authority to rule me. Keep me watchful and prayerful, lest I venture into temptation. And help me say no to both the strongest enticements and the subtlest suggestions of sin.

Amen.

Day 23

In Christ Alone

And because of him you are in Christ Jesus, who
became to us wisdom from God, righteousness
and sanctification and redemption, so that, as it is
written, "Let the one who boasts, boast in the Lord."
(1 Corinthians 1:30–31)

EVERYTHING WE NEED FOR THE PURSUIT of spiritual transformation is found in Christ alone. John MacArthur, in his excellent book *Our Sufficiency in Christ,* tells three rather unusual stories, that are (I think) all true and all illustrate this truth. First, there is the story about two brothers in New York City who were sons of a famous doctor. Both were bachelors, but well educated and lived on the luxurious family estate left to them by their father. They were forgotten over time, because they were recluses. In 1947 the police got an anonymous phone tip that someone had died in the mansion. What the police found were two corpses in a house full of junk— 140 tons of garbage! The brothers had been stockpiling the trash for years, collecting everything, throwing away nothing. Though they were immensely wealthy, they had lived in a squalid dump.

The second story is about William Randolph Hearst, a famous and wealthy newspaper publisher who read about several pieces of art he wanted to add to his collection. He sent his agent all over the world looking for the items. Months later, the agent returned and reported that the items had finally been found: in one of Hearst's warehouses! He had purchased the items years before.

The third story is about a poor man who went on a cruise. He saved all that he could to go on the cruise, but had no money left for food. So, he took a suitcase full of peanut butter sandwiches. But as he watched the porters carry trays of delicious, luxurious food, he almost went crazy. After several days he begged for a plate of food, promising the porter to do anything to earn the meal. The porter informed him that if he had a ticket, he could eat as much as he wanted. The food came with the cruise![1]

Each of those stories could serve as parables for believers who look to someone other than Christ and something other than the gospel to change them, satisfy them, and make them new. Wealthy, they live in the squalid trash of sin, rather than enjoy the treasure of Christ and his glory. Hungry, they try to fill their souls with the peanut butter sandwiches of self effort, thinking that they need to add something to God's grace in order to enjoy the fullness of life in Christ. Like William Randolph Hearst, they are on a quest for something which is already theirs!

The gospel tells us that we have everything we need in Christ. His death is ours; we are therefore freed from sin. His resurrection is ours; we thus walk in newness of life. We don't need to add anything to what Christ has done for us. We simply need to believe the gospel and apply it more deeply to our lives.

As John Calvin wrote in this rhapsodic, worshipful passage in the *Institutes of the Christian Religion,*

> We see that our whole salvation and all its parts are comprehended in Christ [Acts 4:12]. We should therefore take care not to derive the least portion of it from anywhere else. If we seek salvation, we are taught by the very name of Jesus that it is "of him" [1 Cor. 1:30]. If we seek any other gifts of the Spirit, they will be found in his anointing. If we seek strength, it lies in his dominion; if purity, in his conception; if gentleness, it appears in his birth. For by his birth he was made like us in all respects [Heb. 2:17] that he might learn to feel our pain [cf. Heb. 5:2]. If we seek redemption, it lies in his passion; if acquittal, in his condemnation; if remission of the curse, in his cross [Gal. 3:13]; if satisfaction, in his sacrifice; if purification, in his blood; if reconciliation, in his descent into hell; if

1 John F. MacArthur, *Our Sufficiency in Christ* (Wheaton, IL: Crossway Books, 1998 reprint) 7-39, 169, 241-242.

mortification of the flesh, in his tomb; if newness of life, in his resurrection; if immortality, in the same; if inheritance of the Heavenly Kingdom, in his entrance into heaven; if protection, if security, if abundant supply of all blessings, in his Kingdom; if untroubled expectation of judgment, in the power given him to judge. In short, since rich store of every kind of good abounds in him, let us drink from this fountain, and from no other.[2]

Reflection Questions

- Which of the three stories in today's reading best describes your life?

- Have you been searching for spiritual power outside of the gospel? Have you been looking for something that is already yours in Christ Jesus?

- Take a few moments to think about the riches that are already yours in Jesus.

Prayer

Heavenly Father,

I'm amazed by that you have blessed me with every spiritual blessing in Christ. Salvation, strength, purity, redemption, reconciliation, newness of life, immortality—they are all mine in him! How can I thank you? Help me live in light of these gospel realities today.

In Jesus' name,

Amen.

---

2 John Calvin, John T. McNeil, ed., Ford L. Battles, trans., *Institutes of the Christian Religion,* Book II, Chap. XVI. 19 (Philadelphia, PA: The Westminster Press, 1960) 527-528.

Day 24

Called to Holiness

> As obedient children, do not be conformed to
> the passions of your former ignorance, but as he
> who called you is holy, you also be holy in all your
> conduct, since it is written, "You shall be holy, for I
> am holy."
>
> (1 Peter 1:14–16)

SALVATION BEGINS, BUT DOES NOT END, with the work of Christ for us. He is our perfect representative, our sinless substitute. By faith, we are declared righteous in Christ. In Christ we are given a new history, identity, and destiny. But this has radical, far-reaching implications for our present lives. God not only works for us, but in us. He not only counts us as holy, he purposes to make us holy— by calling us to holiness and by applying the gospel to our hearts to produce holiness within us.

In the Old Testament, Israel's call to holiness was rooted in God's holy character and redemptive grace. In Leviticus, for example, the Lord says, "You shall be holy to me, for I the LORD am holy and have separated you from the peoples, that you should be mine" (Lev. 20:26). Notice that the command ("you shall be holy to me") is based both on God's holiness ("for I the LORD am holy") and his gracious initiative in making Israel his people ("and have separated you from the peoples, that you should be mine"). Seven times in Leviticus (Lev. 20:8; 21:8, 15, 23; 22:9, 16, 32), God declares himself to be the Lord who sanctifies his people. And only after he has first sanctified his people, does he then command them to sanctify themselves.

So you shall keep my commandments and do them: I am the
LORD. And you shall not profane my holy name, that I may

be sanctified among the people of Israel. I am the LORD who
sanctifies you, who brought you out of the land of Egypt to be
your God: I am the LORD.

(Lev. 22:31–33)

The New Testament picks up the theme of holiness with the same language. Peter says we are "a holy priesthood" (1 Peter 2:5) and "a holy nation, a people for [God's] own possession" (v. 9). And, lifting language straight out of Leviticus, he reshapes the call to holiness around Christ.

Therefore, preparing your minds for action, and being sober-
minded, set your hope fully on the grace that will be brought
to you at the revelation of Jesus Christ. As obedient children,
do not be conformed to the passions of your former ignorance,
but as he who called you is holy, you also be holy in all your
conduct, since it is written, "You shall be holy, for I am holy."

(1 Peter 1:13–16)

Paul also connects every aspect of our salvation to holiness, from the gracious purpose of God's eternal plan, to the cross work of Christ, to the application of his work in our lives by God's Spirit.

- Election—In Ephesians 1:4 he looks backward to God's gracious election, explaining that God chose us in Christ, "before the foundation of the world, that we should be holy and blameless before him."

- The Cross—Then in Ephesians 5 he says Christ loved the church as his bride and gave himself up for her, "that he might sanctify her, having cleansed her by the washing of water with the word, so that he might present the church to himself in splendor, without spot or wrinkle or any such thing, that she might be holy and without blemish" (Eph 5:25–27; *cf.* Col. 1:22).

- The Work of the Spirit—Paul also thanks God for choosing people to be saved through the "sanctification of the Spirit and belief in the truth" and calling them to this salvation through the gospel (2 Thess. 2:13–14).

- God's call—Believers are called "in holiness" (1 Thess. 4:7) and "to a holy calling" (2 Tim. 1:9).

- New Creation—Even the concept of new creation is linked to holiness, as Paul reminds us that the new man is "created after the likeness of God in true righteousness and holiness" (Eph. 4:24).

Spiritual formation, rightly understood, is about the outworking of God's transforming grace as he conforms us to the image of Christ by the power of his Spirit through the renewing of our minds (Rom. 8:29; 2 Cor. 3:18; Rom. 12:1–2).

Reflection Questions

- How do the Scriptures motivate us to live holy lives?

- How can knowing that every aspect of salvation is connected to holiness help you in the pursuit of holiness today?

- What do you think is involved in "renewing" the mind?

Prayer

Father,

You are a holy God and you have called me to imitate your holiness. You have chosen and redeemed me for the purpose of holiness. This is why you gave Jesus to die for me, and your Spirit to indwell me. Transform me by your grace and make me more like Jesus. Help me to live a holy life.

In Jesus' name,

Amen.

Day 25
The Gospel Pattern of Sanctification

> Do not be conformed to this world, but be
> transformed by the renewal of your mind, that by
> testing you may discern what is the will of God,
> what is good and acceptable and perfect.
> (Romans 12:2)

GOD CALLS US TO HOLINESS or Christlikeness. But how does he actually make us holy? *Only through the gospel.* "Holiness," said John Owen, "is nothing but the implanting, writing, and realizing of the gospel in our souls."[1] But how does this actually work?

Holiness is not mere morality, but the deep, personal transformation of the soul *through* the renewal of the mind in the truth of the gospel. When Paul refers to the stunning contrast between what we once were and who we now are, he grounds the dramatic change we have experienced in our personal appropriation of Christ. We see this in Ephesians 4 as Paul urges his readers not to live as unbelievers who are calloused in soul and have "given themselves up to sensuality, greedy to practice every kind of impurity" (v. 19). Why? Because, "that is not the way you learned Christ!" (v. 20). Paul continues, "assuming that you have heard about him and were taught in him, as the truth is in Jesus, to put off your old self, which belongs to your former manner of life and is corrupt through deceitful desires, and to be renewed in the spirit of your minds, and to put on the new self, created after the likeness of God in true righteousness and holiness" (Eph. 4:21–24).

To urge us to live distinct and separate lives, Paul reminds us of the implications of the message we embraced when we learned,

---

1 John Owen, *A Discourse Concerning the Holy Spirit,* in William H. Gould, ed., *The Works of John Owen,* vol. 3 (Carlisle, PA: The Banner of Truth Trust, 1967 reprint of 1850-53 edition) 370-371.

heard about, and were taught in Christ. We were taught to put off the old self—the old human nature, the personality dominated by sin, inherited from our original father, the first man, Adam. This nature belonged to our former way of life and was characterized by ongoing corruption.

But we were also taught to be renewed in the spirit of our minds. We need inner renewal because our minds are so deeply infected with the deceit of evil (*cf.* vv. 17–18, 22). Transformation is impossible apart from our internalization of gospel truth.

If you own a computer, you've probably had at least one awful experience with a virus. Your computer has been hacked. A virus has contaminated your system. Spyware is compromising your information. A Trojan horse is interfering with your programs. Once you've experienced this electronic nightmare, you know that the only way to combat future infections is regularly to download new or updated antivirus software and scan your computer for threats. If you don't do this, your computer will get infected and eventually lock down or crash. Our minds are much the same. Sin has infected our thinking with viruses, worms, and Trojan horses. Our minds are sabotaged by false patterns of thinking, by deceitful desires, and by images, information, and ideologies that distort reality, compromise truth, and lead to futility. The only way to be freed from this deception is to be continually renewed with the truth of gospel.

And Paul further says that we were taught to put on the new self. If the old self refers to the old, corrupt nature, which is inherited from and patterned after the first man, then the new self refers to the new nature, given to us in the new creation work of God. The new self is human nature renewed, patterned after the perfect, holy humanity of Jesus, the Last Man. It is the new nature and new identity granted to us by God, the new man recreated in his perfect image.

Now notice how the gospel works itself out in Christian living in both negative and positive ways: negatively, in putting off the old; and positively, in putting on the new. As mentioned in previous chapters, God's work in our lives has both once-and-for-all, definitive aspects, but also ongoing, practical, developmental aspects. We see this pattern here as well. Putting off and putting on happens *decisively* when we come to Christ in faith. But the *outworking* of this basic pattern in personal life continues, as Paul builds on this gospel foundation with the brick and mortar of ethical instruction (Eph. 4:25–32). In just seven verses, he presents a series of practical exhortations that address the everyday sins of telling lies, getting angry, stealing, speaking sinfully, and harboring bitterness.

The goal is never simply refraining from sin, but actively replacing sin with righteousness as we are consciously motivated by the gospel. The restoration of God's image within us always has both these negative and positive dimensions. We must put off the old *and* put on the new—put sin to death *and* grow in grace. This is the invariable pattern of Scripture. Theologians call these negative and positive dimensions to holiness "mortification" and "vivification." While it's not important to remember these terms, it is essential that to grasp the biblical concepts. This is how the gospel is realized and written in our souls.

This pattern was set in the death and resurrection of Christ. Through faith in him, we share in his death and resurrection. We have died to sin and now live in newness of life (Rom. 6). But that pattern of death and resurrection is worked out in our lives in the disciplines of mortification and vivification. Killing sin and growing in grace summarize the biblical prescription for a holy life. The table below shows how the gospel is applied to our hearts in the pursuit of holiness.

DEATH	RESURRECTION
We died with Christ (Rom. 6:2–4)	We walk in newness of life (Rom. 6:4)
Put off the old man (Col. 3:9)	Put on the new man (Col. 3:10)
Cleanse yourselves from defilement of body and spirit (2 Cor. 7:1)	Bring holiness to completion in the fear of God (2 Cor. 7:1)
Do not be conformed (Rom. 12:2)	Be transformed (Rom. 12:2)
Crucify the flesh (Gal. 5:24)	Walk in the Spirit (Gal. 5:25)

Continued . . .

DEATH	RESURRECTION
Renounce ungodliness and worldly passions (Titus 2:12)	Live sober, righteous, and godly lives in the present age (Titus 2:12)
Lay aside every weight and sin (Heb. 12:1)	Run the race set before us (Heb. 12:1)
Do not be conformed to the passions of your former ignorance (1 Peter 1:14)	But as he who called you is holy, you also be holy in all your conduct (1 Peter 1:15)
Mortification: Kill your sins	Vivification: Grow in grace

Reflection Questions

- How is this basic pattern of sanctification for a believer established in the death and resurrection of Christ?

- Think about your own life. Are there sins that need to be killed? Are there places where you need to grow in grace?

- Ask God to help you apply the cross to your sins and the resurrection to your need for growth. Then pursue holiness in the power of his grace.

Prayer

Father in Heaven,

I confess that I often fail to live in light of the gospel. Christ has dealt the death blow to my sin, but sometimes I live as if I were still its slave. This should never be! Help me to reckon myself dead to sin and alive in Christ, and in that knowledge, to put sin to death and live in righteousness. Strengthen me by your Spirit.

In Jesus' name,

Amen.

Day 26

Killing Sin

So then, brothers, we are debtors, not to the
flesh, to live according to the flesh. For if you live
according to the flesh you will die, but if by the
Spirit you put to death the deeds of the body, you
will live. For all who are led by the Spirit of God are
sons of God.

(Romans 8:12–14)

*"The tiger ate her hand. It slowly proceeded to eat the
rest of her arm." That's how Vikram Chari described the
horrifying spectacle that he and his six-year-old son
witnessed at the San Francisco Zoo on December 22, 2006,
when a Siberian tiger named Tatiana attacked her keeper.
For those who work with wild animals, the bloody assault
was a reminder of what they already know but don't always
remember— the creatures they've become so accustomed to
can turn on them at any moment. "If you're not afraid of it,
it will hurt you," said animal behaviorist Dave Salmoni. "You
can't get the wild out of a cat because he's in a cage."[1]*

LOTS OF US THINK WE CAN TAME SIN, but, like a tiger, sin turns
and masters us at the first opportunity. You cannot get the wild out of
sin simply by caging it. We may think we have evil under control, that
we have tamed sin, rendering it harmless enough to share a peaceful,
mutual coexistence. But sin will never be domesticated. It is wolf,
not dog; piranha, not goldfish. Evil is untamable. It is our enemy—
opposed to us in every way. At every moment, sin is wired to destroy.

---

1 Adapted from Patricia Yollin, "Horrified zoogoer recalls tiger attack," *The San Francisco
Chronicle,* Monday, January 1, 2007. Available online at: http://www.sfgate.com/
cgi-bin/article.cgi?f=/c/a/2007/01/01/MNG3CNB93Q1.DTL&feed=rss.news. Accessed
August 17, 2008.

The analogy with wild animals breaks down, however, for sin can be far more subtle in its destructive intentions than a slashing claw or crushing jaws. Sin regularly assaults us, though we often fail to notice. Sin knows us well and quietly gnaws away our faith and affections. We can therefore never be tolerant or open-minded about our sin. We are called to aggressively hate our sin—to despise it, reject it, deplore it, starve it, and make every effort to kill it. As the seventeenth-century pastor and theologian John Owen said, "Be killing sin or it will be killing you."[2]

As we saw in the last reading, the biblical prescription for living a holy life can be summarized in two complementary responsibilities: killing sin (mortification) and growing in grace (vivification). The clearest biblical language about mortification is found in Romans 8:12–14 (see the reading above), Colossians 3:5–10, and Galatians 5:24.

Put to death therefore what is earthly in you: sexual immorality, impurity, passion, evil desire, and covetousness, which is idolatry. On account of these the wrath of God is coming. In these you too once walked, when you were living in them. But now you must put them all away: anger, wrath, malice, slander, and obscene talk from your mouth. Do not lie to one another, seeing that you have put off the old self with its practices and have put on the new self, which is being renewed in knowledge after the image of its creator.

(Col. 3:5–10, emphasis added)

And those who belong to Christ Jesus have crucified the flesh with its passions and desires.

(Gal. 5:24, emphasis added)

Simply put, mortification is killing sin. This includes putting to death both the sinful actions (deeds) and sinful motivations (passions and desires) which produce them. But this language of putting to

---

2 John Owen, *The Mortification of Sin: Abridged and made easy to read by Richard Rushing* (Carlisle, PA: The Banner of Truth Trust, 2004) 5.

death does not suggest finality. There is nothing we can do in this life to bring sin to a *complete* end. The imagery of mortification is intended, rather, to communicate the vehemence, enmity, and total-war mentality we must have toward sin.

Mortification is not a once-for-all act, like justification. It is an inseparable component of our ongoing transformation that is a *process* that continues throughout our lives. We "put sin to death," therefore, whenever we consciously recognize sin for the implacable enemy it is, habitually fight its impulses, and weaken its power in our lives—a little bit at a time, day after day, every day, for the rest of our lives.

Reflection Questions

- Do you treat sin like a pet or like a dangerous wild animal?

- As a Christian, you can never declare a cease-fire with sin. Sin is your enemy. Are you fighting?

- Read again the list of sins in Colossians 3. Are any of these sins evident in your life? Ask God for the strength to put them to death.

Prayer

Too often I have treated sin as if it were a plaything instead of the enemy of my soul. Forgive me, Father. Help me see my sins for the dangerous beasts that they really are. And help me resolve to put my sins to death, whatever the cost. For the sake of Jesus, whose death has freed me from my sin, Amen.

Day 27
Taking God's Side Against Sin

Let not sin therefore reign in your mortal body, to make you
obey its passions. Do not present your members to sin as
instruments for unrighteousness, but present yourselves to
God as those who have been brought from death to life, and
your members to God as instruments for righteousness.
(Romans 6:12–13)

TO MORTIFY SIN, YOU MUST LEARN to always take God's side against
your sin. This is implied in yielding ourselves to God (Rom. 6:12–
13; 12:1); but we must be conscious and consistent in *acting on*
the inclinations toward holiness and *acting against* the inclinations
toward sin. "The duty of mortification consists in a constant taking
part with grace, in its principles, actings, and fruits, against the
principle, actings, and fruits of sin."[1]

Every day we are faced with split-second choices. When provoked
by mistreatment, will I indulge my anger and retaliate with angry
words of my own? A cold shoulder? A dirty look? Or I will I respond
in love, with gentleness and grace?

When confronted with a sexually provocative image, will I indulge
in lustful thoughts? Or will I turn away and seek to fill my mind with
the pure pleasures of God? Will I pray for the people represented
in these images, eternal beings made in the image of God? Or will
I reduce them to objects of desire for my own sinful pleasure?

When weighted with responsibilities, will I run through every
worrisome and self-reliant scenario, imagining preventions, escapes,
options? Or will I cast my anxious thoughts on the Lord and

---

1 John Owen, *A Discourse Concerning the Holy Spirit,* in William H. Gould, ed., *The Works
of John Owen,* vol. 3 (Carlisle, PA: The Banner of Truth Trust, 1967 reprint of 1850-53
edition) 548.

prayerfully make my requests known to him, trusting in his wise and merciful providence to rightly order the circumstances of my life?

The only way to mortify sin is to act with increasing consistency on the right inclinations instead of the wrong ones. This is the discipline of ongoing repentance. As John Stott writes,

> The first great secret of holiness lies in the degree and the decisiveness of our repentance. If besetting sins persistently plague us, it is either because we have never truly repented, or because, having repented, we have not maintained our repentance. It is as if, having nailed our old nature to the cross, we keep wistfully returning to the scene of its execution. We begin to fondle it, to caress it, to long for its release, even to try to take it down again from the cross. We need to learn to leave it there. When some jealous, or proud, or malicious, or impure thought invades our mind we must kick it out at once. It is fatal to begin to examine it and consider whether we are going to give in to it or not. We have declared war on it; we are not going to resume negotiations. We have settled the issue for good; we are not going to re-open it. We have crucified the flesh; we are never going to draw the nails.[2]

Reflection Questions

- Do you consistently act against the inclinations of sin? Do you take God's side against your sin?
- Is there any area of life where you need to renew repentance today? Have you in any way resumed negotiations with sin?

---

2 Stott, *The Message of Galatians*, 151-152.

Prayer

Lord Jesus,

I am not my own. I am bought with a price. You have purchased me and I am yours. I therefore yield myself to you. Take my hands and feet, my thoughts and words, indeed, my very self, and use me for your glory. Help me to take your side against every inclination to sin. And empower me by your Spirit.

I ask this in your holy name,

Amen.

Day 28

Replacing Sin with Grace

Put to death therefore what is earthly in you: sexual
immorality, impurity, passion, evil desire, and
covetousness, which is idolatry. On account of these
the wrath of God is coming. In these you too once
walked, when you were living in them. But now you
must put them all away: anger, wrath, malice, slander,
and obscene talk from your mouth. Do not lie to one
another, seeing that you have put off the old self with its
practices and have put on the new self, which is being
renewed in knowledge after the image of its creator. . . .
Put on then, as God's chosen ones, holy and beloved,
compassionate hearts, kindness, humility, meekness,
and patience, bearing with one another and, if one has
a complaint against another, forgiving each other; as
the Lord has forgiven you, so you also must forgive.
And above all these put on love, which binds everything
together in perfect harmony.
(Colossians 3:5–10, 12–14)

REPENTANCE INVOLVES not just turning *from*, but turning *to*.
Holiness demands both "putting off" and "putting on." We must not
only *put off* sin, we must *put on* grace. The negative must be replaced
with the positive.

Owen shows that this is "the great way of the mortification
of sin":

> This, therefore, is the first way whereby the Spirit of God
> mortifieth sin in us; and in a compliance with it, under his
> conduct, do we regularly carry on this work and duty,—that
> is, *we mortify sin by cherishing the principle of holiness*

and sanctification in our souls, labouring to increase and strengthen it by growing in grace, and by a constancy and frequency in acting of it in all duties, on all occasions, abounding in the fruits of it. Growing, thriving, and improving in universal holiness, is the great way of the mortification of sin. The more vigorous the principle of holiness in us, the more weak, infirm, and dying will be that of sin. The more frequent and lively are the actings of grace, the feebler and seldomer will be the actings of sin. The more we abound in the "fruits of the Spirit," the less shall be concerned in the "works of the flesh." And we do deceive ourselves if we think sin will be mortified on any other terms.[1]

As an effective and practical way to apply this to the sins you are fighting, determine to kill each specific sin by cultivating the particular virtue which best counters it. Counter greed by cultivating contentment and generosity. Wage war on pride by practicing humility. Kill lust by loving others in selfless purity. Crucify self-centeredness by serving those around you.

In John Bunyan's allegorical *Holy War*, the members of Diabolus' horde who had subverted the rule of Emmanuel in the city of Mansoul are put on trial. Their names are Mr. Atheism, Mr. Hard-heart, Mr. False-peace, Mr. No-truth, Mr. Pitiless, and Mr. Haughty. Bunyan, who clearly understood the counteracting effect of corresponding virtues, named some of the members of the jury: Mr. Belief, Mr. True-heart, Mr. Upright, Mr. See-truth, Mr. Good Work, and Mr. Humble. The only way truly to get rid of vice—and not just temporarily deflect it—is to displace it with virtue.[2]

---

1 Owen, *A Discourse Concerning the Holy Spirit, in The Works of John Owen*, vol. 3, 552. Emphasis added.

2 John Bunyan, *The Holy War* (Ross-shire, Scotland: Christian Focus Publications, 1993) Chapter Nine.

Reflection Questions

- What are your areas of greatest temptation? What are some specific things you can do, not merely to avoid committing those sins again, but to weaken sin's hold?
- How will you replace your sinful thought patterns and behaviors with those which are virtuous and Christlike?

Prayer

Heavenly Father,

Thank you for rescuing me from sin. Help me today to not only put off the works of the flesh, but to put on the character of Christ. Help me replace evil thoughts with holy thoughts, hurtful words with godly words, and sinful deeds with good works. Clothe me in the perfect character of your Son, in whose name I pray.

Amen.

Day 29

Look to the Cross

> But far be it from me to boast except in the cross
> of our Lord Jesus Christ, by which the world is
> crucified to me, and I to the world.
> (Galatians 6:14)

THE ONLY WAY TO KILL SIN is to look to the cross. Without this all other strategies will ultimately fail. "There is no death of sin without the death of Christ"[1] said Owen. This cross-centered approach to killing sin is clear in Scripture. Before Paul speaks of putting to death the deeds of the body in Romans 8:13, he reminds us that:

> *There is therefore now no condemnation for those who are in Christ Jesus. For the law of the Spirit of life has set you free in Christ Jesus from the law of sin and death. For God has done what the law, weakened by the flesh, could not do. By sending his own Son in the likeness of sinful flesh and for sin, he condemned sin in the flesh, in order that the righteous requirement of the law might be fulfilled in us, who walk not according to the flesh but according to the Spirit.*
> *(Romans 8:1–4)*

Let's trace the argument. The righteous requirement of the law can be fulfilled in us (v. 4), only because: we are in Christ Jesus (v. 1); absolved from guilt and condemnation (v. 1); and are freed from the law of sin and death (v. 2) through the sin-defeating death of God's Son (v. 3).

Paul goes on in this passage to point out that, since we now live according to the Spirit rather than the flesh, we have our minds set

---

1 Owen, *The Mortification of Sin*, 41.

on the Spirit (vv. 5–6). The Spirit of God dwelling within in us proves we belong to Christ and that our bodies will be resurrected like his (vv. 9–11). Therefore, we are not to live as debtors to the flesh. Instead we are put to death the misdeeds of the body, by the power of God's Spirit (vv. 12–13).

A similar dynamic is at work in Colossians 3 and Romans 6. In Colossians 3, the apostle points us back to the fact that we have been raised with Christ (v. 1), that we have died (v. 3a), that our life is hidden with Christ in God (v. 3b), and that when Christ appears, we will also appear with him in glory (v. 4). Paul is reminding us of our union with Christ in the gospel realities of his death, burial, resurrection, and exaltation. Only then does he tell us to put sin to death (v. 5). And in Romans 6:9–13, in chapter five, the power to say no to sin comes from Christ's decisive defeat of sin in his death.

Over and over again, when the Bible commands us to put sin to death, it does so in the context of Christ's victory over the very sins we battle. Because of the death and resurrection of Jesus, we fight from a position of victory. Therefore, as Owen reminds us:

> Set your faith upon Christ for the killing of your sin. His blood is the great sovereign remedy for sin-sick souls. . . . By faith fill your heart with a right consideration of the provision that God has made in the work of Christ for the mortification of your sins.[2]

But the cross is also what progressively frees the affections of our hearts from the enticements of sin. Paul said, "But far be it from me to boast except in the cross of our Lord Jesus Christ, by which the world is crucified to me, and I to the world" (Gal. 6:14). Commenting on this verse, Owen writes,

> Set your affections on the cross of Christ. This is eminently effective in frustrating the whole work of indwelling sin. The apostle gloried and rejoiced in the cross of Christ. His heart was set on it. It crucified the world to him, making it a dead

---

2 Owen, 116-117.

and undesirable thing (Gal. 6:14). The baits and pleasures of sin are all things in the world, "the lust of the flesh, the lust of the eyes, and the pride of life." By these, sin entices and entangles our souls. If the heart is filled with the cross of Christ, it casts death and undesirability on them all, leaving no seeming beauty, pleasure, or comeliness in them. Again, Paul says, "It crucifies me to the world and makes my heart, my affections, and my desires dead to all these things. It roots up corrupt lusts and affections, and leaves no desire to go and make provision for the flesh to fulfill its lusts." Labour, therefore, to fill your hearts with the cross of Christ.[3]

Reflection Questions

- Have you been trying to fight sin without meditating on the cross of Christ? How is that going for you?

- Think about your greatest moments of temptation. How would you handle these temptations differently if the sight of Christ crucified for those very sins was carved into your mind?

- What are some practical strategies you can use to fill your heart with the cross of Christ?

Prayer

Father in Heaven,

I have nothing to boast in apart from the cross of Jesus Christ. When I consider his thorn-crowned brow, his nail-pierced hands, his wounded side, my heart melts. How can I sin against such love? Fill my heart with thoughts of Christ crucified and bind me to you with heart-purifying love.

Amen.

---

3 John Owen, *Indwelling Sin in Believers: Abridged and Made Easy to Read* (Carlisle, PA: The Banner of Truth Trust, 2010) 99–100.

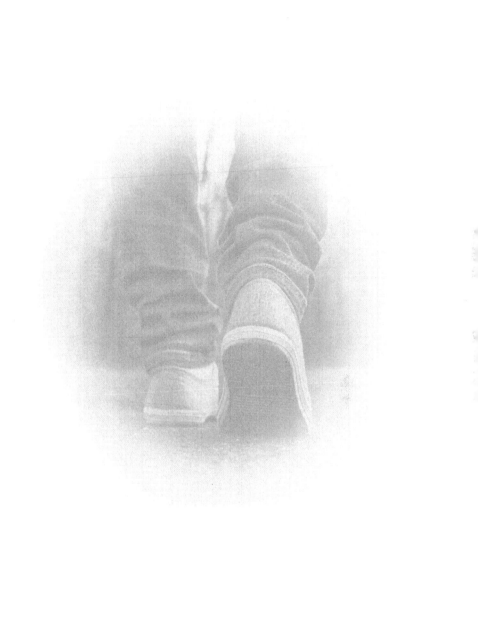

Day 30

Life Out of Death

Truly, truly, I say to you, unless a grain of wheat falls into
the earth and dies, it remains alone; but if it dies, it bears
much fruit. Whoever loves his life loses it, and whoever
hates his life in this world will keep it for eternal life.

(John 12:24–25)

C. S. LEWIS' *THE GREAT DIVORCE* is a fantasy about a busload of
shadowy, hellish ghosts who are given an excursion into the solid
borderland of Heaven. Here, the tangible weight of God's glory is
evident in every blade of grass, and fruit so heavy the ghosts can
scarcely lift a single piece. Each phantom is given opportunity to stay
in the borderland and develop the capacities for savoring the higher
joys of Heaven. But one by one, they choose to return to the Gray
City (Hell) rather than loose themselves of the passions, desires, and
sins that enslave them.

All except for one, a wraith who is afflicted with lust, which
is embodied as a red lizard that sits on his shoulder, whispering
seductive lies. A strong, fiery angel offers to kill the lizard but the
wraith produces every reason imaginable for allowing it to live.
He fears the pain of the angel's blazing hand. He imagines that the
destruction of his lust will be his personal undoing as well.

Finally, he agrees to let the angel seize the lizard and break its
neck. When the reptile is destroyed, the shadowy wraith suddenly
becomes solid, while the dead lizard morphs into a vibrant stallion.
With unbounded joy, the new man mounts his steed and rides into
the heavenly country.[1]

---

1 C. S. Lewis, *The Great Divorce* (New York, NY: HarperOne, 1946, 1973) Chapter Eleven.
Perhaps I should add that the point of Lewis' story (and my use of it) is not that post-
mortem salvation is possible, but that love for sin is what bars us from the enjoyment
of heavenly pleasures.

This is a picture of what can happen when we are diligent in putting to sin to death. The battle is not *against* our joy and happiness, but *for* our maximum pleasure—pleasure in God. The fight may be painful. It will involve giving up evil things that are presently dear to us. But when the battle is finished and the sin is mortified, God brings life—new, transforming, unexpectedly wonderful, joyful life—out of death.

The old and tired is put off, the fresh and new is put on. God changes weakness into strength. He transforms our broken desires into something larger, more beautiful, and more powerful than we could ever have imagined. And in the power and goodness of those desires, God takes us places we didn't think we could go.

Reflection Questions

- Do you sometimes fear that you will come out the loser in following Jesus? Reflect on Jesus' words in John 12. What does Jesus promise?

- How does Lewis's story inform your imagination when thinking about the sinful passions and desires that you need to kill?

Prayer

Open my eyes that I might behold in your crucified and risen Son the power of life out of death. As Christ was crucified for me, help me now to crucify my sins in conformity to his death. Help me to know him in both the fellowship of his sufferings and the power of his resurrection. Mortify my sins by the power of your Spirit and transform me into the glory image of your Son.

In Jesus' name,

Amen.

Day 31

Learning to Walk

> By this we may know that we are in him: whoever says he abides
> in him ought to walk in the same way in which he walked.
>
> (1 John 2:5b–6)

HOLLY AND I HAVE FOUR CHILDREN, Stephen, Matthew, Susannah, and Abby Taylor. Each one of them has been slow in learning to walk. The children of many of our friends began walking at ten or twelve months, but not ours. Our four are quite verbal, however, picking up words and phrases quickly. Does this mean they will be better communicators than athletes? It wouldn't be a surprise—both Holly and I are sadly lacking in coordination! That's okay. Not all people can be quick on their feet.

But what's okay in human development is not nearly so okay in the Christian life. Like my children, believers usually learn to "talk" before they can "walk." They pick up Christian lingo quickly. Even as new converts, Christians can often spout Bible verses, debate theology, and pray in Christianese. Learning to walk in obedience, however, is a slower process. And genuine spiritual growth is not measured in how well we talk, but in how faithfully we walk with Jesus.

The word *walk* is an important one in Scripture, for it stands "at the center of Paul's ethical thinking."[1] In Ephesians, Paul describes our behavior prior to salvation as *walking* in trespasses and sins (Eph. 2:1). A few verses later, he says we are created in Christ Jesus to *walk* in good works (Eph. 2:10). The last three chapters of Ephesians are structured around five uses of the word *walk*.

---

1 Klyne Snodgrass, *The NIV Application Commentary: Ephesians* (Grand Rapids, MI: Zondervan, 1996) 96.

- We should *walk* in a manner worthy of God's call, by relating to one another with humility, gentleness, patience, forbearance, and love (4:1–2).

- We should "no longer *walk* as the Gentiles do, in the futility of their minds," since we have put off the old self and put on the new (4:17–24).

- We should be imitators of God and *walk* in love as Christ loved us (5:1–2).

- We should *walk* in light, since we are children of light, not darkness (5:8).

- We should look carefully how we *walk*, being wise, not unwise (5:15).

The metaphor of walking teaches us three important things about spiritual growth. It is a lifelong, active, imitation of Jesus.

Lifelong. First, *walk* underscores the lifelong nature of spiritual growth. This is a recurring emphasis in this book. Spiritual formation doesn't happen over a long weekend, but through the course of many months and years. The Christian life is not a hundred-yard dash, but the journey of a lifetime.

Active. Second, growing in grace requires our participation and effort. As Dallas Willard writes, "Grace is opposed to earning, but not to effort."[2] We are saved by grace, not meritorious works. But that doesn't mean we are passive in our transformation. Children must learn to walk as they develop and mature into healthy adults. So must we.

Imitation. Third, Jesus is the example we follow. We imitate Jesus by walking in love (Eph. 5:2; *cf.* Rom. 6:4; Col. 2:6; 1 John 2:6). His life is the pattern for ours. For a moment, think of a dance instead of a walk, a dance gracefully choreographed to music. You can only learn the moves by imitating the choreographer. Spiritual formation is similar.

---

2 Dallas Willard, *The Great Omission: Reclaiming Jesus' Essential Teachings on Discipleship* (San Francisco, CA: HarperSanFrancisco, 2006) 76.

As new believers, we don't know the right moves. Even as we begin to learn them, we can't execute them smoothly. We're not sure on our feet yet. We don't really know how to dance. We need to continue imitating the one who knows the dance perfectly and can execute it without flaw. This is Jesus, who has perfectly choreographed the Christian life for us. As we imitate him and copy his steps, we learn to dance . . . to walk as he walked.

Reflection Questions

- What three things does the metaphor of walking teach us about spiritual growth?

- Have you been too passive in your spiritual growth? Where do you need to apply effort in the pursuit of transformation?

- Think about the character of Jesus—his compassion, humility, purity, love, and joy. What specific aspects of his character can you seek to imitate today?

Prayer

Help me, gracious Father, to walk as Jesus walked. Help me learn from him how to live. Show me where I need to grow and enable me to exert holy effort in seeking to imitate your Son.

Amen.

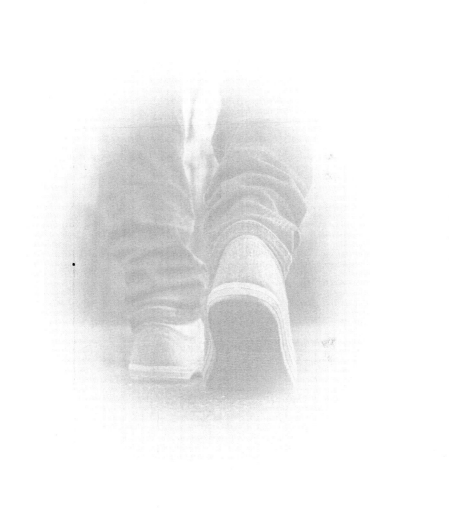

Day 32

Renewing the Mind

> I appeal to you therefore, brothers, by the mercies of
> God, to present your bodies as a living sacrifice, holy
> and acceptable to God, which is your spiritual worship.
> Do not be conformed to this world, but be transformed
> by the renewal of your mind, that by testing you may
> discern what is the will of God, what is good and
> acceptable and perfect.
> (Romans 12:1–2)

SPIRITUAL TRANSFORMATION is a process of inner renewal that involves the total reorientation of our minds and hearts. This is one of the key differences between religion and true Christ-centered change. God is interested in more than external conformity to a set of rules. He wants to make us new on the inside. The change he desires goes much deeper than behavior. Our minds must be renewed.

Deep, lasting change requires me to attend to how this present age impacts my thinking. "Do not be conformed to this world, but be transformed by the renewal of your mind" (v. 2). Rather than conforming to the mindset of the fallen world around me, I must be renewed in the core of my being. The capacity to discern and embrace God's will for healthy, God-honoring humanity depends on the transformation of my thoughts and affections. God changes me not by manipulating my choices or forcing my will, but by restoring my heart and renovating my mind. The implications for spiritual formation are profound. J.I. Packer observes,

> Man was made to know good with his mind, to desire it,
> once he has come to know it, with his affections, and to
> cleave to it, once he has felt its attraction, with his will; the
> good in this case being God, his truth and his law. God

accordingly moves us, not by direct action on the affections
or will, but by addressing our mind with his word, and so
bringing to bear on us the force of truth. . . . Affection may
be the helm of the ship, but the mind must steer; and the
chart to steer by is God's revealed truth.[1]

This means we are *transformed* as our minds are *informed*. Since this is true, it is vital to saturate our minds with the truth of the gospel. Jesus said as much, when he prayed to his Father, "Sanctify them in the truth; your word is truth" (John 17:17). Only when the truth is renewing our minds, will we be transformed, and thus be equipped "by testing [to] discern what is the will of God, what is good and acceptable and perfect" (Rom. 12:2).

As believers, we long for a resource that will help us grow. We want to discern God's will and follow it. So we look to counselors, seminars, and books in our quest for the silver bullet, the secret of change, the key to victory. But the most important resource—the truth of the gospel—is at arm's reach. We only have to appropriate it in our lives. Spiritual growth is not about moving on from where we began—the gospel. It's about growing deeper in the gospel. Or, rather, getting the gospel deeper into us. As Richard Lovelace writes,

Growth in faith is the root of all spiritual growth and is
prior to all disciplines of works. True spirituality is not a
superhuman religiosity; it is simply true humanity released
from bondage to sin and renewed by the Holy Spirit. This is
given to us as we grasp by faith the full content of Christ's
redemptive work: freedom from the guilt and power of sin,
and newness of life through the indwelling and outpouring
of his Spirit.[2]

---

1 J. I. Packer, *A Quest for Godliness: The Puritan Vision of the Christian Life* (Wheaton, IL: Crossway Books, 1990) 195.
2 Richard F. Lovelace, *Dynamics of Spiritual Life: An Evangelical Theology of Renewal* (Downers Grove, IL: Inter-Varsity Press, 1979) 19-20.

Reflection Questions

- Why is renewing the mind so crucial in the process of spiritual transformation?

- How is the mind transformed and renewed? What is the instrument God uses to renew our minds?

- If renewing the mind depends on saturating the mind with the truth of the gospel, what are some practical and strategic ways you could do that?

Prayer

Sanctify me, Father, in the truth. Your word is truth. Fill me with your truth. Let the word of Christ dwell richly in my heart. Renew my mind and transform my thoughts, affections, motives, and desires. Help me to saturate my mind with the truth of the gospel today.

In Jesus' name,

Amen.

Day 33

Depending on the Spirit

> And we all, with unveiled face, beholding the glory
> of the Lord, are being transformed into the same
> image from one degree of glory to another. For this
> comes from the Lord who is the Spirit.
> (2 Corinthians 3:18)

IS THE RESPONSIBILITY for spiritual growth left in my hands? If the gospel is what changes me and it's up to me to apply it, does this cast me back upon myself? Look again at what Paul says 2 Corinthians 3:18: "And we all, with unveiled face, beholding the glory of the Lord, are being *transformed* into the same image from one degree of glory to another. *For this comes from the Lord who is the Spirit*" (emphasis added). The agent of transformation is the Spirit of the Lord. The power comes from him.

Spiritual growth depends on saturating our minds with truth, but transformation is not merely a cognitive process. It is personal and supernatural. "Spiritual life is produced by the presence and empowering of the Holy Spirit, not simply by the comprehension of doctrinal propositions or strategies of renewal."[1]

So, does that mean there is nothing for us to do? Not at all. For Paul also commands us to "walk by the Spirit" (Gal. 5:16, 22), and "be filled with the Spirit" (Eph. 5:18). There is, you see, a dynamic interplay between God's work and ours. The Spirit empowers all of our obedience, yet it is still our responsibility to "keep in step with the Spirit" (Gal. 5:25, NIV). Once again, Paul's words help us.

---

1 Richard F. Lovelace, *Dynamics of Spiritual Life: An Evangelical Theology of Renewal* (Downers Grove, IL: Inter-Varsity Press, 1979) 79.

Therefore, my beloved, as you have always obeyed, so now, not only as in my presence but much more in my absence, work out your own salvation with fear and trembling, for it is God who works in you, both to will and to work for his good pleasure.

(Phil. 2:12–13)

This exhortation captures the interaction. We are given responsibility: "work out your own salvation" (v. 12). But we are *not* left on our own. The command to work out our salvation is grounded in God's promise to work in us. This work of God is on two levels: our motivations and our actions.

To Will: Motivations. "For it is God who works in you, both *to will* and to work for his good pleasure" (v. 13, emphasis added). To "will" is to desire, determine, or resolve. The original word embraces both the affections and volitions of the human personality: God works on our desires and choices. John MacArthur suggests that God uses two things to work on our wills: holy discontent and holy aspirations.[2] He makes us dissatisfied with our sinfulness and inspires spiritual longings for something better. He changes the motivational structures of our hearts. J. I. Packer calls this "life supernaturalized at the motivational level,"[3] for any desire within us for true holiness has come from God, not ourselves.

To Work: Actions. "For it is God who works in you, both to will and *to work* for his good pleasure" (v. 13, emphasis added). To "work" means to operate, effect, or do. God gives us not only new desires but also the ability to carry them out. This is why Paul teaches us to pray that God would fulfill our resolves for good and our works of faith by his power (2 Thess. 1:11).

---

2 John F. MacArthur, *Our Sufficiency in Christ* (Wheaton, IL: Crossway Books, 1998 reprint) 207-208.
3 J. I. Packer, *Rediscovering Holiness* (Ann Arbor, MI: Vine Books, 1992) 103.

So, we have a responsibility. We must work out our own salvation. We must obey. We must put sin to death, fight the good fight of faith, grow in grace, and pursue holiness. Yet we can only obey God *as we are empowered by the grace of his Spirit.*

I have a casual appreciation for classical music and a particular admiration for Beethoven's Ninth Symphony. Every time I listen to it, I am moved by its magnificent beauty. I admire Beethoven's talent. But to suggest that I could compose a symphony just as majestic is ridiculous. Admiration is one thing; imitation is another. Sometimes we feel the same way about following Jesus. We admire the perfection of his holy humanity—but imitate him? This seems out of reach. But what if someone discovered a way of replicating Beethoven's genius in me? What if I could have Beethoven himself composing and conducting music through my hands? Then I *could* write a symphony!

This is the role the Spirit plays in our lives! He lives inside of us as the "Spirit of Christ" (Rom. 8:9). Jesus lived the exemplary Spirit-filled life. His character is precisely what God aims to produce in us. The Lord Jesus is our pattern. And his Spirit, sent into our hearts, is the agent who works from the inside out to reproduce this pattern in our lives. We will not grow if we are left to ourselves. We must depend on the Spirit. Since this is true, let us heed the counsel of Richard Lovelace:

We should make a deliberate effort at the outset of every day to recognize the person of the Holy Spirit, to move into the light concerning his presence in our consciousness and to open up our minds and to share all our thoughts and plans as we gaze by faith into the face of God. We should continue to walk throughout the day in a relationship of communication and communion with the Spirit mediated through our knowledge of the Word, relying upon every office of the Holy Spirit's role as counselor mentioned in Scripture. We should acknowledge him as the illuminator of truth and of the glory of Christ. We should look to him as teacher, guide, sanctifier, giver of assurance concerning our

*sonship and standing before God, helper in prayer, and as
the one who directs and empowers witness.*[4]

Reflection Questions

- What is the biblical balance of grace and effort? Do you see
how we are commanded to obey, but can only obey as God
strengthens us with the grace of his Spirit?

- Do you regularly ask God to empower you by his Spirit?

- Take a few moments now (and every day) to ask for the
Spirit's help. Remember, you can do nothing without him.

Prayer

*I am weak, Lord, but you are strong. Without you I can
do nothing, but I can do all things through Christ who
strengthens me. I ask you to enlighten my mind, change
my heart, and strengthen my will by the illuminating,
heart-transforming, power of your Spirit. Help me to obey
you, even as I know you are working within me to desire
obedience in the first place.*

I ask this for Jesus' sake,

Amen.

---

4 Lovelace, 131.

Day 34

Growing Down

Blessed are the poor in spirit, for theirs is the kingdom of heaven.
(Matthew 5:3)

ARE YOU DISCOURAGED as you consider your present level of spiritual maturity? Are you stumbling in your walk with Jesus? Are you in greater need now than when you began this book? As painful as it may be, this awareness is actually a sign of health. G. C. Berkouwer rightly observed that "the life of sanctification proceeds in weakness, temptation, and exposure to the powers of darkness."[1] This is normal spiritual growth.

C. S. Lewis once wrote that "when a man is getting better, he understands more and more clearly the evil that is still left in him." Surely this is why Paul, near the end of his life, confessed himself the foremost of sinners (1 Tim. 1:15). However, as Lewis went on to say, "When a man is getting worse, he understands his own badness less and less. A moderately bad man knows he is not very good; a thoroughly bad man thinks he is alright."[2] Knowing you are not all right is a good indication that you are on the road to recovery. Spiritual maturity leads us to greater humility. The process of growing up turns out to be a process of growing down.

John Newton, author of the well-loved hymn "Amazing Grace," discovered this as well. In lyrics that echo the story of Jonah, Newton wrote:

I asked the Lord that I might grow
In faith, and love, and every grace,
Might more of his salvation know,
And seek more earnestly his face.

---

1 G. C. Berkouwer, *Faith and Sanctification* (Grand Rapids, MI: Wm. B. Eerdmans Publishing Co., 1962) 66.
2 C. S. Lewis, *Mere Christianity* (San Francisco, CA: HarperSanFrancisco, 1952) 93.

I hoped that in some favoured hour
At once He'd answer my request,
And by His love's constraining power
Subdue my sins, and give me rest.

Instead of this, He made me feel
The hidden evils of my heart;
And let the angry powers of hell
Assault my soul in every part.

Yea more, with His own hand
He seemed intent to aggravate my woe;
Crossed all the fair designs I schemed,
Blasted my gourds, and laid me low.

"Lord why is this," I trembling cried,
"Wilt thou pursue thy worm to death?"
"'Tis in this way," the Lord replied,
"I answer prayer for grace and faith."

"These inward trials I employ,
From self and pride to set thee free
And break thy schemes of earthly joy,
That thou may'st find thy all in Me."[3]

If the pace of your growth in Christ is slower than you would like, don't be too discouraged. Let your sense of need drive you to his feet. Seeing your need to grow up is the first step to actually doing so.

Reflection Questions

- What causes you to feel discouragement in your spiritual life? How should you respond to discouragement, in light of today's reading?

- Make a list of your current spiritual needs. Don't be discouraged with the length of the list. Just take your needs to Jesus in prayer right now.

---

3 John Newton, "Prayer Answered by Crosses," 1779.

Prayer

"I need thee every hour, most gracious Lord." I am only beginning to understand just how desperate my need for you really is. Without you I can do nothing. Help me to embrace the humbling truth about myself. But let it lead me not to discouragement or despair but to greater dependence on you and your grace.

Amen.

Day 35

The Holy Pursuit of Joy

The joy of the LORD is your strength . . .
(Nehemiah 8:10)

EVERYONE LONGS FOR HAPPINESS. And believers in Jesus thirst for holiness. But holiness and happiness are not mutually exclusive. God is not a cosmic killjoy who is indifferent to the joy of his children! To suggest that God doesn't want us to be happy rips the heart out of biblical commands such as "Delight yourself in the LORD, and he will give you the desires of your heart" (Ps. 37:4) and "Make a joyful noise to the LORD, all the earth! Serve the LORD with gladness! Come into his presence with singing!" (Ps. 100:1–2).

God is concerned with both our holiness and our joy. On one hand, God knows we can never find true and lasting happiness apart from holiness, because holiness is the pure oxygen that happiness breathes. Without holiness, joy suffocates, withers, and dies. Sin kills joy. But when we cherish righteousness and detest sin, joy will flourish and grow. As Scripture says of Jesus, "You have loved righteousness and hated wickedness; therefore God, your God, has anointed you with the oil of gladness beyond your companions" (Heb. 1:9). In the words of Thomas Brooks, an English pastor in the seventeenth century, "Holiness differs nothing from happiness but in name. Holiness is happiness in the bud, and happiness is holiness at the full. Happiness is nothing but the quintessence of holiness."[1]

---

1 Thomas Brooks, *The Crown and Glory of Christianity, or Holiness the Only Way to Happiness,* in Alexander B. Grosart, ed., *The Works of Thomas Brooks,* vol. 4 (Carlisle, PA: The Banner of Truth Trust, 2002 reprint of 1861-67 edition) 37.

On the other hand, the quest for joy is one of the primary motivations for pursuing holiness. Over and over, Scripture appeals to our desire for joy and satisfaction by promising blessing for those who seek Christ. And Scripture repeatedly warns that misery will come to those who refuse Christ and choose sin instead. Seeking satisfaction outside of a relationship with God simply won't work. As C. S. Lewis wrote,

> God made us: invented us as a man invents a machine. A car is made to run on petrol, and it would not run properly on anything else. Now God designed the human race to run on Himself. He Himself is the fuel our spirits were designed to burn, or the food our spirits were designed to feed on. There is no other. That is why it is just no good asking God to make us happy in our own way without bothering about religion. God cannot give us happiness and peace apart from Himself, because it is not there. There is no such thing.[2]

Only as we seek our satisfaction in God will we begin to break free from the gravitational pull of sin's lower pleasures. In the words of Matthew Henry, "The joy of the Lord will arm us against the assaults of our spiritual enemies and put our mouths out of taste for those pleasures with which the tempter baits his hooks."[3]

Reflection Questions

- Why are happiness and holiness not mutually exclusive? What is the relationship between holiness and joy?

- Why does seeking satisfaction in sin instead of God never work? How can knowing this change your whole outlook on sin and sanctification?

---

2 C. S. Lewis, *Mere Christianity* (San Francisco, CA: HarperSanFrancisco, 1952) 50.
3 Quoted in John Piper, *Desiring God: The Meditations of a Christian Hedonist* (Sisters, Oregon: Multnomah Books, Third Edition, 2003) 12.

Prayer

You, Father, make known to me the path of life. In your presence there is fullness of joy and at your right hand are pleasures forevermore. Satisfy me today with your steadfast love and arm me against the assaults of the enemy by giving me greater joy in you than I could ever find in sin.

Amen.

Day 36

The Sanctifying Power of Faith

> By faith Moses, when he was grown up, refused to be
> called the son of Pharaoh's daughter choosing rather to
> be mistreated with the people of God than to enjoy the
> fleeting pleasures of sin. He considered the reproach of
> Christ greater wealth than the treasures of Egypt, for he was
> looking to the reward.
> (Hebrews 11:24–26)

ONE OF THE MOST COMPELLING biblical examples of how faith in God's promises empowers holiness is found in the story of Moses as told in Hebrews 11.

The writer to the Hebrews presents Moses as an example of faith. Faith is characterized by the conviction that God will reward those who seek him. "And without faith it is impossible to please him, for whoever would draw near to God must believe that he exists and that he rewards those who seek him" (Heb. 11:6). It is impossible to please God if you seek him out of any other motive than the desire for reward. We do not seek God as his benefactors, thinking we can reward him. We are always the beneficiaries of his grace.

Notice the decisions and actions Moses' faith produced. We see him both refusing and choosing. By faith Moses "refused to be called the son of Pharaoh's daughter." Imagine the implications of this! Moses had been raised in the household of Pharaoh. He was "instructed in all the wisdom of the Egyptians, and he was mighty in his words and deeds" (Acts 7:22). He was a prince in Egypt— possibly a high-ranking government official. As part of the royal family, he had luxury at his fingertips: the choicest food, the richest accommodations, the most beautiful women. And he turned his back on all of it. He "refused to be called the son of Pharaoh's daughter choosing rather to be mistreated with the people of God than to enjoy the fleeting pleasures of sin" (vv. 24–25).

How could he do this? Why did he consider "the reproach of Christ greater wealth than the treasures of Egypt"? Verse 26 answers: "For he was looking to the reward". Moses was empowered by the promise of a superior satisfaction. "By faith he left Egypt, not being afraid of the anger of the king, for he endured as seeing him who is invisible" (v. 27). He was captivated by a greater beauty, a more enduring treasure, a more satisfying pleasure than Egypt could offer. To quote John Piper:

> Faith is not content with "fleeting pleasures." It is ravenous for joy. And the Word of God says, "In Thy presence is fullness of joy; in Thy right hand there are pleasures forever" (Psalm 16:11). So faith will not be sidetracked into sin. It will not give up so easily in its quest for maximum joy.[1]

That is faith: Believing that God, and all he promises to be for us in the gospel, is more satisfying than sin. Faith is the powerful conviction that joy in Jesus is so superior to the fleeting pleasures of sin that I am compelled to choose the eternal over the temporal and the Savior over sin, even if I suffer.

Reflection Questions

- What does the example of Moses teach us about faith? How does this illustrate Hebrews 11:6?

- What are some of your particular sin struggles right now? How can faith in God's promises help you in the battle?

---

1 John Piper, *The Purifying Power of Living by Faith in FUTURE GRACE* (Sisters, OR: Multnomah Books, 1995) 335.

Prayer

Heavenly Father,

My greatest need is to believe the good promises of your word. When I sin, it is always because of I've believed a lie. Undeceive me, Lord! Help me to see that you are supremely good and that your promises are more than sufficient to meet my needs. Help me to see that the satisfaction you offer in Christ is superior to the fleeting, passing pleasures of sin. Strengthen my faith.

In Jesus' name,

Amen.

Day 37

Training for Godliness

Train yourself for godliness.
(1 Timothy 4:7b)

SUPPOSE YOU WERE TO ASK ME to run with you in a marathon next week. I could say yes, and have every intention of doing so. But I would never make the finish line. My good intentions couldn't possibly compensate for the lack of training. Now if you asked to me to run a marathon that is ten months away, I could do it—if I spent adequate time in training. But trying harder simply wouldn't work because, as John Ortberg observes, "There is an immense difference between training to do something and trying to do something."[1]

Respecting the distinction between training and merely trying is the key to transformation in every aspect of life. People sometimes think that learning how to play Bach at the keyboard by spending years practicing scales and chord progressions is the "hard" way. The truth is the other way around. Spending years practicing scales is the easy way to learn to play Bach. Imagine sitting down at a grand piano in front of a packed concert hall and having never practiced a moment in your life. That's the hard way.[2]

Living the Christian life is about training, not trying. But we often forget this. We try to be patient with our children, to show love to people who irritate us, to refrain from lust when confronted with sensuality, and to not feel anxious about difficult circumstances.

---

1 John Ortberg, *The Life You've Always Wanted: Spiritual Disciplines for Ordinary People* (Grand Rapids, MI: Zondervan, 2002) 43. All of my thinking on training vs. trying, including the marathon illustration, is dependent on Ortberg. His book is a helpful and accessible introduction to spiritual disciplines.
2 Ortberg, 44.

But try as we will, we won't succeed if we haven't strengthened and shaped our souls through spiritual training.

You'll never become like Christ by simply exerting more effort in trying harder to be a better person. You have to develop new capacities in your character. And that requires the power of the Spirit in forming your soul through disciplines. Spiritual disciplines, "those personal and corporate disciplines that promote spiritual growth,"[3] are the means God has given us for training to live as Jesus lived. These practices are called *disciplines* because they involve our deliberate participation in training for the purpose of godliness. They are called *spiritual* disciplines because their effectiveness depends on the gracious work of the Spirit of God.

So, the key word is *train*. As Paul says to Timothy, "*Discipline* yourself for the purpose of godliness" (1 Tim. 4:7, NASB). The Greek word for "discipline" is *gumnazo* (our words gymnastics and gymnasium derive from its root). Translated "train" (ESV, NIV), "exercise" (KJV), and "discipline" (NASB), *gumnazo* was used to describe the intense discipline of athletes in first-century Greco-Roman culture. Competitors in the Olympic or Isthmian games were so relentless in pursuit of a champion's wreath that they trained in the nude, part of a strict environment that eliminated all nonessentials.

The New Testament urges us to adopt a similarly radical regimen in the spiritual life. We are called to discipline our bodies, keeping them under control as we pursue an imperishable crown (1 Cor. 9:24–27). We must strip off "every weight" and the "sin which clings so closely" and run the race set before us (Heb. 12:1). We should forget what is behind and strain forward to what lies ahead as we "press toward the goal for the prize of the upward call of God in Christ Jesus" (Phil. 3:13–14). As we have learned, God's ultimate goal is to glorify himself through transformed human beings. We further that goal as we deliberately engage in practices that train us for godliness. If we're serious about this pursuit, we will train with intensity, like an Olympic athlete.

---

3 Donald S. Whitney, *Spiritual Disciplines for the Christian Life* (Colorado Springs, CO: NavPress, 1991) 15.

Reflection Questions

- Have you ever approached spiritual transformation with the mindset of an athlete? Do you train for godliness?
- Do you consistently integrate spiritual disciplines (such as Bible reading, meditation, and prayer) into your life?

Prayer

Father,

Please help me to set my eyes on the prize—the imperishable crown of life that belongs to those who run the race of faith. Enable me to train myself for godliness, to embrace the call to live a disciplined, self-controlled, and godly life in Christ Jesus. Forgive me for my spiritual indolence. Strengthen me with grace and give me the focus and endurance of an athlete as I run the race set before me. Amen.

Day 38
Receiving versus Achieving

> You then, my child, be strengthened by the
> grace that is in Christ Jesus . . .
> (2 Timothy 2:1)

SPIRITUAL DISCIPLINES are about receiving, not achieving. Using the disciplines wisely does not mean checking things off a religious to-do list. The Pharisee in Luke 18 did that, boasting in his prayers, "I fast twice a week; I give tithes of all that I get." He had two disciplines nailed down, fasting and giving. He thought he had achieved much. But Jesus contrasted this man with a humble and broken tax collector, who wouldn't even lift his eyes to heaven, but pleaded, "God, be merciful to me a sinner!" The tax collector's focus was not on his achievements, but on his deep need for mercy (Luke 18:12–13). Beware of using spiritual disciplines to achieve something with God! The disciplines are not about achieving, but receiving. As Bryan Chapell writes, we should view

> the Christian disciplines as means of opening our mouths
> to breathe in all the loving resources God has already
> provided. Opening my mouth in prayer and praise does
> not manufacture more of God's love for me, any more than
> opening my mouth makes more air. The means of grace
> simply allow me to experience the fullness of the love that
> God has already fully and completely provided.[1]

Do not approach the disciplines as if you are benefiting God or meriting his favor. You are not. When you read or meditate on Scripture, seek the Lord in prayer, worship with the Lord's people, or give yourself to serving others, you come to an overflowing fountain of

---

1 Bryan Chapell, *Holiness by Grace: Delighting in the Joy that is Our Strength* (Wheaton, IL: Crossway Books, 2001) 57.

divine grace. When you come to this fountain, do not bring a cup full of self-sufficiency, thinking you can add something to God's infinite mercy. Come instead with an empty cup of need for God to fill.

In all our consideration and all our practice of the spiritual disciplines, we must remember that only the gospel can change us. Religious practices alone will not. Never be content with the mere forms of piety. Always be feeding your soul at the banqueting table of God's love in Christ! John Owen wrote:

> Let us live in the constant contemplation of the glory of Christ, and virtue will proceed from him to repair all our decays, to renew a right spirit within us, and to cause us to abound in all duties of obedience . . . . The most of our spiritual decays and barrenness arise from an inordinate admission of other things into our minds; for these are they that weaken grace in all its operations. But when the mind is filled with thoughts of Christ and his glory, when the soul thereon cleaves unto him with intense affections, they will cast out, or not give admittance unto, those causes of spiritual weakness and indisposition.[2]

The spiritual disciplines are really all about keeping your heart in the constant contemplation of Christ. Fill your mind with the gospel and cleave to Christ with all your heart. Think of Christ often. Marvel at his incarnation—the Word was made flesh! Meditate on the achievements of the cross and the dying love of Jesus. Celebrate in your soul the resurrection of Christ. Death is defeated once and for all. Stand in awe at the ascension and enthronement of the God-Man, Jesus Christ. God's plan for his image-bearing human beings is restored in Christ. The second Adam reigns! As you soak your mind with the gospel and deeply absorb its truths in your soul, you will be changed.

---

2 John Owen, *Meditations and Discourses Concerning the Glory of Christ; Applied unto Unconverted Sinners and Saints under Spiritual Decays* in William H. Gould, ed., *The Works of John Owen*, vol. 1 (Carlisle, PA: The Banner of Truth Trust, 1967 reprint of 1850-53 edition) 460-461.

Reflection Questions

- Why is the distinction between achieving and receiving important?

- How can you remind yourself regularly of the true purpose of spiritual disciplines: to keep your heart in constant contemplation of Christ?

Prayer

Thank you, Father, for your all-sufficient grace! Help me to live in dependence on your grace this day, to approach every discipline and every duty not as a means of earning or achieving anything in your sight, but as an opportunity to receive fresh supplies of your grace. Fill me by your Spirit with the fullness that is in Christ Jesus.

Amen.

Day 39

Suffering and Glory

For I consider that the sufferings of this present
time are not worth comparing with the glory that
is to be revealed to us.

(Romans 8:18)

PAUL'S REFLECTIONS ON SUFFERING offer a crucial insight into
their purpose: present afflictions actually work for our *future glory.*
Paul's point is that future glory will far outweigh and compensate for
present suffering. But in Second Corinthians he says even more:

*So we do not lose heart. Though our outer self is wasting
away, our inner self is being renewed day by day. For this light
momentary affliction is preparing for us an eternal weight of
glory beyond all comparison, as we look not to the things that
are seen but to the things that are unseen. For the things that are
seen are transient, but the things that are unseen are eternal.*

(2 Cor. 4:16–18)

Paul has a confidence that holds him steady through trials. He
doesn't lose heart, because he knows God will raise him from the
dead, as he did Jesus. He further knows that his afflictions are being
used to extend grace to others and thus increase the thanksgiving and
glory God will receive. This is why he is not discouraged. Though his
body wastes away with affliction, persecution, and probably death,
his inner nature is being renewed (vv. 8–16).

Then in verse 17, Paul says something stunning: "This light
momentary affliction is preparing for us an eternal weight of glory
beyond all comparison." The afflictions will not only be more
than compensated for by glory, they are actually *preparing* glory.
"Preparing" is a common word in the New Testament that means to

produce something. James uses this word when he says "the testing of your faith *produces* steadfastness" (James 1:3). Paul's meaning is unmistakable—there is something about suffering now that results in glory in eternity. As C. S. Lewis said, "They say of some temporal suffering, 'No future bliss can make up for it,' not knowing that Heaven, once attained, will work backwards and turn even that agony into a glory."[1]

This truth teaches us to view our trials as seeds of eternal glory planted in the soil of our present lives. Thinking of difficult circumstances like this doesn't come naturally to us short-sighted, time bound mortals. It's difficult to see past the immediacy of poverty, divorce, cancer, or persecution. But faith in Christ enables us to "look not to the things that are seen but to the things that are unseen" (v. 18).

One of the most helpful word pictures for this comes, once again, from C. S. Lewis:

> Imagine yourself as a living house. God comes in to rebuild
> that house. At first, perhaps, you can understand what He
> is doing. He is getting the drains right and stopping the
> leaks in the roof and so on: you knew that those jobs needed
> doing and so you are not surprised. But presently he starts
> knocking the house about in a way that hurts abominably
> and does not seem to make sense. What on earth is He up
> to? The explanation is that He is building quite a different
> house from the one you thought of—throwing out a new
> wing here, putting on an extra floor there, running up
> towers, making courtyards. You thought you were going
> to be made into a decent little cottage: but He is building a
> palace. He intends to come and live in it Himself.[2]

When we view our afflictions from this perspective, we realize that God is using them to make us into better, more beautiful creatures than we could ever otherwise become. The refiner's fire is hot—but the fire burns away dross and tempers the metal of our

---

1 C. S. Lewis, *The Great Divorce* (New York, NY: HarperOne, 1946, 1973) 69.
2 C. S. Lewis, *Mere Christianity* (New York, NY: HarperOne, 1952, 1980) 205.

faith, making it stronger. God's fatherly discipline does not bring immediate joy—but his rod helps us share his holiness. The palace will not be built as long as the remnants of the cottage stand. The demolition is painful—but this is the price God is willing to pay in preparing us for glory.

Reflection Questions

- What difficulties in life are you facing right now?

- Have you ever recognized that your trials were actually a part of God's plan to make you more like Jesus? Do you find this encouraging?

Prayer

Lord,

I believe, but help my unbelief. Help me to trust you even in the darkness. Help me to embrace your good and wise purposes in suffering and to believe that you will turn my present agony into future glory.

Amen.

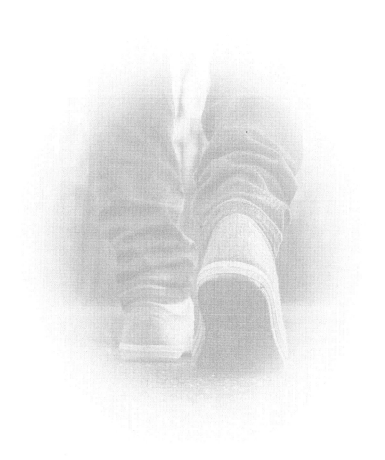

Day 40
Transformation is a Community Project

> Beloved, let us love one another, for love is from God, and
> whoever loves has been born of God and knows God.
>
> (1 John 4:7)

HOW DOES GOD USE RELATIONSHIPS within the body of Christ to help us become more like Jesus? If we are convinced that "grace is conveyed through the body of Christ along horizontal channels as well as through the vertical relationship of each believer to God,"[1] and if we can see *how this happens,* we will be better equipped to cooperate with God in receiving this grace and extending it to others.

In Ephesians 4, Paul spells out the implications of one of the dominant metaphors for the church, that of a body. He tells us that just as a victorious king dispenses the spoils of war to his people, so has the ascended Christ granted gifts to his people. The purpose of these gifts is to build up the body of Christ. And the goal of "body building" is to help us attain to "mature manhood" and "the measure of the stature of the fullness of Christ." Without the "body building" ministry, we will remain immature children, as susceptible to false teaching as boats are to storms at sea (Eph. 4:7–14).

Then Paul gives us the key for how we can together grow into Christ's image.

> *Speaking the truth in love, we are to grow up in every way*
> *into him who is the head, into Christ, from whom the whole*
> *body, joined and held together by every joint with which it is*
> *equipped, when each part is working properly, makes the body*
> *grow so that it builds itself up in love.*
>
> *(Eph. 4:15–16)*

---

1 Lovelace, *Dynamics of Spiritual Life*, 168.

Speaking the truth in love! That's it. To understand what Paul is saying here is to grasp the key to mutual spiritual growth within local churches. As it turns out, however, "'Speaking the truth in love' is not the best rendering of his expression, for the Greek verb makes no reference to our speech. Literally, it means 'truthing . . . in love', and includes the notions of 'maintaining', 'living' and 'doing' the truth."[2]

We might say, therefore, that spiritual maturity is the result of a mutual, loving, truth-oriented ministry. This is "perhaps the most important ethical guideline in the New Testament, one that summarizes what Christian living is about: truth, love, and continual growth into Christ in everything."[3]

This balance of truth-plus-love is crucial. As Tim Chester writes, "Love without truth is like doing heart surgery with a wet fish. But truth without love is like doing heart surgery with a hammer."[4] We must embody truth, not just express it. So truth, fused with love, is incarnated in our lives as we live it out with one another. Paul David Tripp concurs: "God transforms people's lives as people bring his Word to others . . . . The combination of powerful truth wrapped in self-sacrificing love is what God uses to transform people."[5]

This is all well and good, and absolutely true. But let's step back from the theory for a moment to make a practical point: *We cannot grow up through "truthing in love" if we are not together.* The body builds itself up in love as its various parts are "joined and held *together*." A dismembered body does not grow.

Paul emphasizes the interdependence of the members in verse 16 by saying that the body is "joined and held together by every joint with which it is equipped when each part *is working properly*." The body only grows as each part is connected to the whole and communicating with the whole. Only under these circumstances can each individual part fulfill its unique role. Christ, as the head of this spiritual body, endows the church with gifts in order to equip us

---

2 John R. W. Stott, *The Message of Ephesians: God's New Society* (Downers Grove, IL: Inter-Varsity Press, 1979) 172.

3 Klyne Snodgrass, *The NIV Application Commentary: Ephesians* (Grand Rapids, MI: Zondervan, 1996) 206.

4 Tim Chester, *You Can Change* (Nottingham, England: Inter-Varsity Press, 2008) 158.

5 Tripp, *Instruments in the Redeemer's Hands*, 21.

to serve one another. And he supplies each of us with the strength and grace to work properly, each doing his or her part. Growth in spiritual maturity is a matter of mutual cooperation.

Reflection Questions

- Are you involved in a local church? Have you been trying to live the Christian life as a "lone ranger"? Are you going it alone?

- If transformation is a community project, how will you commit yourself to pursuing holiness in partnership with others?

Prayer

Father,

Thank you for the reminder that being your child means belonging to your family. I am not alone and am not meant to live in isolation from others. Grant me renewed understanding of and commitment to the local church. Help me to intentionally cultivate the kinds of relationships with others that will lead to greater likeness to Christ.

In Jesus' name and for his sake,

Amen.

Other books by Brian G. Hedges

Active Spirituality: Grace and Effort in the Christian Life
(Shepherd Press)

Christ All Sufficient: An Exposition of Colossians
(Shepherd Press)

*Christ Formed in You: The Power of the Gospel for Personal
Change* (Shepherd Press)

Christ Formed in You: The Study Guide (Shepherd Press)

Hit List: Taking Aim at the Seven Deadly Sins
(Cruciform Press)

Licensed to Kill: A Field Manual for Mortifying Sin
(Cruciform Press)

The Story of His Glory (Crossway)

Thriving in Grace: 12 Ways the Puritans Fuel Spiritual Growth
(co-authored with Joel R. Beeke) (Reformation Heritage Books)

Watchfulness: Recovering a Lost Spiritual Discipline
(Reformation Heritage Books)

With Jesus: Finding Your Place in the Story of Christ
(Shepherd Press)

Books edited by Brian G. Hedges

Comfort and Holiness from Christ's Priestly Work
by William Bridge (Reformation Heritage Books)

The Cure for Unjust Anger by John Downame
(Reformation Heritage Books)

Gospel Evidences of Saving Faith by John Owen
(Reformation Heritage Books)

Holy Helps for a Godly Life by Richard Rogers
(Reformation Heritage Books)